teach yourself®

instant spanish

elisabeth smith

For over 60 years, more than 50 million people have learnt over 750 subjects the **teach yourself** way, with impressive results.

be where you want to be with **teach yourself**

For UK order enquiries: please contact Bookpoint Ltd, 130 Milton Park, Abingdon, Oxon OX14 4SB. Telephone: +44 (0) 1235 827720. Fax: +44 (0) 1235 400454. Lines are open 09.00–17.00, Monday to Saturday, with a 24-hour message answering service. Details about our titles and how to order are available at www.teachyourself.co.uk

For USA order enquiries: please contact McGraw-Hill Customer Services, PO Box 545, Blacklick, OH 43004-0545, USA. Telephone: 1-800-722-4726. Fax: 1-614-755-5645.

For Canada order enquiries: please contact McGraw-Hill Ryerson Ltd, 300 Water St, Whitby, Ontario L1N 9B6, Canada. Telephone: 905 430 5000. Fax: 905 430 5020.

Long renowned as the authoritative source for self-guided learning – with more than 50 million copies sold worldwide – the **teach yourself** series includes over 500 titles in the fields of languages, crafts, hobbies, business, computing and education.

British Library Cataloguing in Publication Data: a catalogue record for this title is available from the British Library.

Library of Congress Catalog Card Number: on file.

First published in UK 1998 by Hodder Education, 338 Euston Road, London, NW1 3BH.

First published in US 1998 by The McGraw-Hill Companies, Inc.

2nd edition published 2003. 3rd edition published 2006.

The **teach yourself** name is a registered trade mark of Hodder Headline.

Copyright © 1998, 2003, 2006 Elisabeth Smith.

Typeset by Transet Limited, Coventry, England.
Printed in Great Britain for Hodder Education, a division of Hodder Headline, 338 Euston Road, London, NW1 3BH, by Cox & Wyman Ltd, Reading, Berkshire.

Hodder Headline's policy is to use papers that are natural, renewable and recyclable products and made from wood grown in sustainable forests. The logging and manufacturing processes are expected to conform to the environmental regulations of the country of origin.

Impression number 10 9 8 7 6 5 4 3 2
Year   2010 2009 2008 2007 2006

contents

4 contents

read this first

If, like me, you usually skip introductions, don't! Read on! You need to know how **Instant Spanish** works and why.

When I decided to write the **Instant** series I first called it *Barebones*, because that's what you want: *no frills, no fuss, just the bare bones and go!* So in **Instant Spanish** you'll find:

- Only 393 words to say, well ... nearly everything.

- No ghastly grammar – just a few useful tips.

- No time wasters such as 'the pen of my aunt...'.

- No phrase book phrases for when you take Flamenco lessons in Bilbao.

- No need to be perfect. Mistakes won't spoil your success.

I've put some 30 years of teaching experience into this course. I know how people learn. I also know how long they are motivated by a new project (a few weeks) and how little time they can spare to study each day ($^{1}/_{2}$ hour). That's why you'll complete **Instant Spanish** in six weeks and get away with 35 minutes a day.

Of course there is some learning to do, but I have tried to make it as much fun as possible, even when it is boring. You'll meet Tom and Kate Walker on holiday in Spain. They do the kind of things you need to know about: shopping, eating out and getting about. As you will note Tom and Kate speak **Instant Spanish** all the time, even to each other. What paragons of virtue!

To get the most out of this course, there are only two things you really should do:

- Follow the **Day-by-day guide** as suggested. Please don't skip bits and short-change your success. Everything is there for a reason.
- If you are a complete beginner, buy the recording that accompanies this book. It will help you to speak faster and with confidence.

When you have filled in your **Certificate** at the end of the book and can speak **Instant Spanish,** I would like to hear from you. Why not visit my website www.elisabeth-smith.co.uk, e-mail me at elisabeth.smith@hodder.co.uk, or write to me care of Hodder Education, 338 Euston Road, London, NW1 3BH?

Elisabeth Smith

how this book works

Instant Spanish has been structured for your rapid success. This is how it works:

Day-by-day guide Stick to it. If you miss a day, add one.

Dialogues Follow Tom and Kate through Spain. The English of Weeks 1–3 is in 'Spanish-speak' to get you tuned in.

New words Don't fight them, don't skip them – learn them! The **Flash cards** will help you.

Good news grammar After you read it you can forget half and still succeed! That's why it's good news.

Flash words and flash sentences Read about these building blocks in the **Flash card** section on page 92. Then use them!

Learn by heart Obligatory! Memorizing puts you on the fast track to speaking in full sentences.

Let's speak Spanish *You* will be doing the talking – in Spanish.

Spot the keys Listen to rapid Spanish and make sense of it.

Say it simply Learn how to use plain, **Instant Spanish** to say what you want to say. Don't be shy!

Test your progress Mark your own test and be amazed by the result.

Answers This is where you'll find the answers to the exercises.

▶ This icon asks you to switch on the recording.

Pronunciation If you don't know about it and don't have the recording go straight to page 15. You need to know about pronunciation before you can start Week 1.

Progress chart Enter your score each week and monitor your progress. Are you going for *very good* or *outstanding*?

Certificate It's on the last page. In six weeks it will have your name on it!

progress chart

At the end of each week record your test score on the progress chart below.

At the end of the course throw out your worst result – anybody can have a bad week – and add up your *five* best weekly scores. Divide the total by five to get your average score and overall course result. Write your result – *outstanding, excellent, very good* or *good* – on your **certificate** at the end of the book.

If you scored more than 80% enlarge it and frame it!

Progress chart

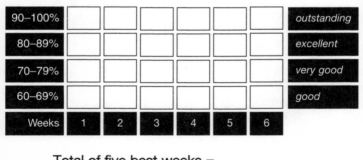

90–100%							outstanding
80–89%							excellent
70–79%							very good
60–69%							good
Weeks	1	2	3	4	5	6	

Total of five best weeks =

divided by five =

Your final result _____ %

01

week one

Day zero

- Open the book and read **Read this first!**
- Now read **How this book works**.

Day one

- Read **In the aeroplane**.
- Listen to/Read **En el avión**.
- Listen to/Read the **New words**, then learn some of them.

Day two

- Repeat **En el avión** and the **New words**.
- Listen to/Read **Pronunciation**.
- Learn more **New words**.
- Use the **Flash words** to help you.

Day three

- Learn all the **New words** until you know them well.
- Read and learn the **Good news grammar**.

Day four

- Cut out and learn the ten **Flash sentences**.
- Listen to/Read **Learn by heart**.

Day five

- Listen to/Read **Let's speak Spanish**.
- Revise! Tomorrow you'll be testing your progress.

Day six

- Listen to/Read **Let's speak more Spanish** (optional).
- Listen to/Read **Let's speak Spanish – fast and fluently** (optional).
- Translate **Test your progress**.

Day seven is your day off!

day-by-day guide

In the aeroplane

Tom and Kate Walker are on their way to Spain. They are boarding flight QS 915 to Malaga via Barcelona and squeeze past Pedro Iglesias. (*The English of Weeks 1–3 is in 'Spanish-speak' to get you tuned in.*)

Tom   Excuse me, we have the seats four a and four b.

Pedro   Ah, yes, a moment please.

Tom   Hello, how are you? We are Tom and Kate Walker.

Pedro   Good morning, I call myself (My name is) Iglesias.

Tom   Julio Iglesias?

Pedro   No, come off it! My name is Pedro Iglesias.

Tom   We are going to Malaga. And you?

Pedro   No, I am going to Barcelona but I am from Seville.

Tom   Seville? I was in Seville in May – for my company.

Pedro   In what do you work?

Tom   I work with computers.

Pedro   And you, Mrs Walker?

Kate   Well... I have worked in Mobil three years. Now I work in Rover.

Pedro   Are you from London?

Kate   No, we are from Manchester. We have been one year in New York and two years in London. Now we work in Birmingham.

Pedro   I have worked four years in Seat but now I work in the Bank of Spain.

Tom   And how is the work in the bank? Is it good?

Pedro   The work is boring but the pay is better. I have a house big, a Mercedes and four children. My wife is American from Los Angeles and she has a girlfriend in Dallas. She talks always with her on the telephone and goes always to Los Angeles. It costs a lot of money.

Kate   And are you now also on holiday?

Pedro   No, unfortunately not. We have always the holidays in September. We are going to Mallorca but without the children. We have a house in Palma without telephone, and we go there without mobile!

▶ En el avión

Tom and Kate Walker are on their way to Spain. They are boarding flight QS 915 to Malaga via Barcelona and squeeze past Pedro Iglesias.

Tom	Perdone, tenemos los asientos cuatro a y cuatro b.
Pedro	¡Ah! sí, un momento por favor.
Tom	Hola, ¿Qué tal? Somos Tom y Kate Walker.
Pedro	Buenos días. Me llamo Iglesias.
Tom	¿Julio Iglesias?
Pedro	No, ¡qué va! Me llamo Pedro Iglesias.
Tom	Nosotros vamos a Málaga. ¿Y usted?
Pedro	No, yo voy a Barcelona pero soy de Sevilla.
Tom	¿Sevilla? He estado en Sevilla en mayo – para mi empresa.
Pedro	¿En qué trabaja?
Tom	Trabajo con ordenadores.
Pedro	¿Y usted, Señora Walker?
Kate	Pues... yo he trabajado en Mobil tres años. Ahora trabajo en Rover.
Pedro	¿Es de Londres?
Kate	No, somos de Manchester. Hemos estado un año en Nueva York y dos años en Londres. Ahora trabajamos en Birmingham.
Pedro	Yo he trabajado cuatro años en Seat pero ahora trabajo en el Banco de España.
Tom	¿Y qué tal el trabajo en el banco? ¿Es bueno?
Pedro	El trabajo es aburrido pero el sueldo es mejor. Tengo una casa grande, un Mercedes y cuatro niños. Mi mujer es americana, de Los Ángeles, y tiene una amiga en Dallas. Habla siempre con ella por teléfono y va siempre a Los Ángeles. Cuesta mucho dinero.
Kate	¿Y está ahora también de vacaciones?
Pedro	No, desgraciadamente no. Tenemos siempre las vacaciones en septiembre. Vamos a Mallorca, pero sin los niños. Tenemos una casa en Palma sin teléfono, ¡y vamos allí sin móvil!

▶ New words

Learning words the traditional way can be boring. If you enjoy the **Flash cards** why not make your own for the rest of the words. Always say the words OUT LOUD. It's the fast track to speaking!

en   in / on
el, la, los, las   the
el avión   the aeroplane
perdón, perdone   excuse me
tenemos   we have
los asientos   the seats
cuatro   four
a, b   pronounced 'uh', 'bay'
y   and
sí   yes
un momento   a moment
por favor   please
hola   hello
¿qué tal?   how are you, how is…?
somos   we are
buenos días   good day, good morning
me llamo   my name is…
no   no, not
¡qué va!   come on! (expression)
nosotros   we
vamos   we go, we are going, let's go!
a/al   to, to the
usted/ustedes   you (one person) / you (more than one person)
yo   I
voy   I go, I am going
pero   but
soy   I am
de/del   from, of / from, of the
he estado   I have been, I was
mayo   May
para   for
mi   my
la empresa   the company

qué   what
trabaja   he/she/it works, you work
trabajo   I work, also: (the) work
con   with
ordenador/es   computer/s
señora   Mrs, woman
pues…   well…, well then
he trabajado   I have worked
tres   three
el año, los años   the year, the years
ahora   now
es   you are, he/she/it is
hemos estado   we have been, we were
un, una   a, one
dos   two
trabajamos   we work
el Banco de España   the Bank of Spain
bueno/a   good
aburrido/a   boring
el sueldo   the pay, salary
mejor   better
tengo   I have
una casa / en casa   a house / at home
grande   big
los niños   the children
la mujer   the woman, wife
americana   American
tiene   he/she/it has, you have
una amiga   a girlfriend
habla   he/she/it speaks, you speak
siempre   always
ella   she, her

por teléfono *on the telephone*	de vacaciones *on holiday(s)*
va *he/she/it goes, you go*	**desgraciadamente** *unfortunately*
cuesta/cuestan *it costs /*	**septiembre** *September*
they cost	**sin** *without*
mucho/a *much, a lot*	**el (teléfono) móvil** *the mobile*
el dinero *the money*	*(phone)*
está *he/she/it is, you are*	**allí** *there*
también *also*	

> **TOTAL NEW WORDS: 78**
> ...only 315 words to go!

Some easy extras

los meses (the months)

enero, febrero, marzo, abril, mayo, junio, julio, agosto, septiembre, octubre, noviembre, diciembre

números (numbers)

cero,	**uno,**	**dos,**	**tres,**	**cuatro,**	**cinco,**	**seis,**	**siete,**	**ocho,**	**nueve,**	**diez**
0	1	2	3	4	5	6	7	8	9	10

More greetings

buenas tardes *(good afternoon)*, **buenas noches** *(good night)*, **hasta luego** *(bye, until later)*, **adiós** *(good bye, for longer absence)*.

▶ Pronunciation

The Spanish language is beautiful, so drop all inhibitions and try to speak **Spanish** – not English with the words changed…!

If Spanish pronunciation is new to you please buy the recording. But if you are good at languages, or would like a refresher, here are the rules:

1 Vowels

The word in brackets gives you an example of the sound. Say the sound OUT LOUD and then the Spanish examples OUT LOUD.

a	(*star*)	casa, Málaga, días, vamos
e	(*best*)	es, pero, bueno, teléfono
i	(*seat*)	sí, sin, mi, días, asientos
o	(*not*)	no, con, somos, momento
u	(*June*)	un, usted, cuesta, mucho

All vowels are pronounced separately: bu–e–no, asi–en–tos, e-u-ro

2 Consonants

h	(-)	This is not pronounced at all: hola, he, hemos, habla, ahora
j	(*loch*)	Like the guttural sound in the Scottish word loch: julio, trabajo, mujer
ll	(*yes/million*)	It is a bit of each. When you say me llamo the ll sounds like a y, but when you say calle it's more like the lyer sound in million. If your tongue gives up, stay with the y. Say: allí, Sevilla
ñ	(*canyon*)	Watch out when you see the little wriggle on the top of the n: año, niño (say **anyo, ninyo**) España
qu	(*kettle*)	qué, quince (15), quinientos (500)
r		Give this a vigorous, throaty roll: aburrrrido...
z	(*this*)	The moment you spot a z, it's a lisp: cerveza (*beer*), izquierda (*left*), trozo (*piece*)

c + e or i	(*theft*)	This is a lisp!: Barcelona, cinco, desgraciadamente
c + any other letter	(*cut, clear*)	Just like in English: casa, con, cuatro, claro
g + e or i	(*loch*)	It's back to the throaty ch of loch! Luckily there are only two **Instant** words with ge or gi: gente and colegio
g + any other letter	(*go, gust*)	Just like in English: grande, golf, guapo

3 The accent

You stress the second syllable from the end: mo-**men**-to, tra-**ba**-jo, **va**-mos, te-**ne**-mos, or-de-na-**do**-res. But when there's an accent, stress that part: a-**llí**, te-**lé**-fo-no.

Congratulations for having worked through the rules of pronunciation!

▶ Good news grammar

This is the **Good news** part of each lesson. Remember, I promised: *no ghastly grammar!* Every week I explain just a few things and talk you through the differences between English and Spanish. This will help you to speak Spanish **Instantly**.

1 Names of things – nouns

There are two kinds of nouns in Spanish: masculine and feminine.
You can tell which is which by the word **el** or **la**, or **un** or **una** in front of the word. You can also tell by the ending of the noun.

Words ending in **-o** are masculine: **el dinero** or **un banco**.
Words ending in **-a** are feminine: **la casa** or **una amiga**.

The adjective describing a noun also ends in **-o** or **-a**. So *the good bank* becomes **el banco bueno**. *A good house* becomes **una casa buena**.

Unfortunately, not all nouns and adjectives behave so obediently. Some nouns end in any old letter: **la mujer** or **la televisión** (*the TV*), and some adjectives, like **grande**, do not change. And then there is **el día,** just to confuse you!

But these non-conformists are in the minority, so most of the time you can get it right ... **el banco bueno** ... **una amiga buena**.

When there is more than one thing (plural) **el** becomes **los**. All the rest just add an s: **los bancos buenos, las amigas buenas**.

Good news: If you get muddled and say **los casas buenos,** nobody is going to throw a fit. Everyone will understand you perfectly!

2 Doing things – verbs

This is a bit of bad news in Spanish, so brace yourself!
Unlike the English, the Spanish do not use *I, you, he, she, it, we,* or *they* to identify *who* is doing something unless they wish to clarify or stress it. So most of the time the only way you can tell *who is doing something* is by the *verb itself*.

Each person has his/her own form of verb ending, but sometimes an ending is shared. This could lead to some confusion, but amazingly it usually works out all right.

There are a handful of verbs which you'll need every day. Spend ten minutes on each. **Trabajar** belongs to the Good Verbs Team. Team members have the same endings. Know one – know all!

	trabajar *(to) work*		tener *(to) have*	
(yo)	trabaj<u>o</u>	*I work*	tengo	*I have*
(usted)	trabaj<u>a</u>	*you work*	tiene	*you have*
(él)	trabaj<u>a</u>	*he, it works*	tiene	*he, it has*
(ella)	trabaj<u>a</u>	*she, it works*	tiene	*she, it has*
(nosotros)	trabaj<u>amos</u>	*we work*	tenemos	*we have*
(ellos, ellas)	trabaj<u>an</u>	*they work*	tienen	*they have*
(ustedes)	trabaj<u>an</u>	*you work*	tienen	*you have*

(Usted) **trabaja** – (ustedes) **trabajan**: **trabaj<u>a</u>** is used when talking to one person, **trabaj<u>an</u>**, when talking to more than one. Spanish has two other words for *you*: **tú** and **vosotros**. These are informal and familiar and need extra endings. You don't need them for **Instant Spanish** – just use **usted** and **ustedes** or the verb form that goes with them. **¿Trabaja, Kate? ¿Trabajan, Tom y Kate?** Are you shell-shocked? Will you remember all these endings? Don't worry! By Week 3 it will be a piece of cake!

3 Asking questions

Es bueno. *It is good.* **¿Es bueno?** *Is it good?* You simply use your voice to turn a statement into a question.

▶ Learn by heart

Don't be tempted to skip this exercise because it reminds you of school… If you want to **speak**, not stumble, saying a few lines by **heart** does the trick! Learn **Me llamo** by heart after you have filled in the gaps with your personal, or any, information.

Example **Me llamo** Sarah Lawson. **Soy de** Newcastle.

When you know the lines by heart, go over them again until you can say them aloud fluently and fairly fast. Can you beat 40 seconds? Excellent! Give **Me llamo** a bit of life. You'll remember it better that way.

Me llamo…

Me llamo ....(*name*).
Soy de ....(*place*).
He estado en ....(*place*) en.................... (*month*).
He trabajado en......................................(*name of firm*) tres años.
Ahora trabajo en...(*name of firm*).
Tengo una casa en..................................(*place*) y cuesta mucho.
En agosto vamos a ....(*place*).
¿Qué tal Marbella en enero, bueno o aburrido?

▶ Let's speak Spanish

I shall give you ten English sentences and you'll put them into Spanish. Always speak OUT LOUD. After each one check the answer at the bottom of this page. Tick it if you got it right. If you have the recording, listen to check your answers to **Let's speak Spanish**.

1 Hello, my name is Walker.
2 Are you from London?
3 Yes, I am from London.
4 We are going home. Bye!
5 I work with Pedro in Palma.
6 Do you have a Mercedes?
7 No, unfortunately not.
8 We have a house in Marbella.
9 How is the work, good?
10 Boring, but the pay is good.

Well, how many did you get right? If you are not happy, do them again.

Here are some questions in Spanish and you are going to answer in Spanish. Answer the first five with **sí**, and talk about yourself. In questions 16–20 I am talking to you and your friend. Say **sí** and 'we'.

11 ¿Es de Bristol?
12 ¿Tiene una casa en Londres?
13 Pepe va a Granada. ¿Y usted?
14 ¿Tiene teléfono?
15 ¿Trabaja con ordenadores?
16 Vamos a casa. ¿Y ustedes?
17 Trabajamos en Los Ángeles. ¿Y ustedes?
18 Tenemos amigos en Málaga. ¿Y ustedes?
19 Vamos a Sevilla. ¿Y ustedes?
20 Tenemos un trabajo aburrido. ¿Y ustedes?

Answers

1 Hola, me llamo Walker.
2 Es de Londres?
3 Sí, soy de Londres.
4 Vamos a casa. ¡Hasta luego!
5 Trabajo con Pedro en Palma.
6 ¿Tiene un Mercedes?
7 No, desgraciadamente, no.
8 Tenemos una casa en Marbella.
9 ¿Qué tal el trabajo, bueno?
10 Aburrido, pero el sueldo es bueno.
11 Sí, soy de Bristol.
12 Sí, tengo una casa en Londres.
13 Sí, voy a Granada.
14 Sí, tengo teléfono.
15 Sí, trabajo con ordenadores.
16 Sí, vamos a casa.
17 Sí, trabajamos en Los Ángeles.
18 Sí, tenemos amigos en Málaga.
19 Sí, vamos a Sevilla.
20 Sí, tenemos un trabajo aburrido.

Well, what was your score? For 20/20 give yourself a triple gold star!

▶ Let's speak more Spanish

Here are some optional exercises. They may stretch the 35 minutes a day by an extra 15 minutes. But the extra practice will be worth it.

And always remember: near enough is good enough!

In your own words

This exercise will teach you to express yourself freely. Use only the words you have learned so far.

Tell me in your own words that...

Example   you are Peter Smith
Soy Peter Smith.

1 you originate from Manchester
2 you have an American friend
3 you are a workaholic... (you work much)
4 but you don't have a lot of cash
5 you have two children
6 the children are six and eight (have six and eight years)
7 unfortunately you work with a PC; it's boring
8 your wife works for a company in Bath
9 you own a property in Valencia
10 you have a holiday in April

Answers

1 Soy de Manchester.
2 Tengo un amigo americano / una amiga americana.
3 Trabajo mucho...
4 pero no tengo mucho dinero.
5 Tengo dos niños.
6 Los niños tienen seis y ocho años.
7 Desgraciadamente trabajo con un ordenador; es aburrido.
8 Mi mujer trabaja para una empresa en Bath.
9 Tengo una casa en Valencia.
10 Tengo las vacaciones en abril.

► Let's speak Spanish – fast and fluently

No more stuttering and stumbling! Get out the stopwatch and time yourself with this fluency practice.

Translate each section and check if it is correct, then cover up the answers and say the three or four sentences fast!

20 seconds per section for a silver star, 15 seconds for a gold star.

Some of the English is in 'Spanish-speak' to help you.

Good evening. I am going to Madrid. You, too?
No, I work in Madrid – in a bank. Now I am going to Salamanca.
I have the holidays – without the computer.

Buenas noches. Voy a Madrid. ¿Usted también?
No, trabajo en Madrid – en un banco. Ahora voy a Salamanca.
Tengo las vacaciones – sin el ordenador.

How is Salamanca? Is it big?
It is not big, but it is not boring.
And it does not cost a lot.
I have a girlfriend, Carmen.

¿Qué tal Salamanca? ¿Es grande?
No, no es grande, pero no es aburrida.
Y no cuesta mucho.
Tengo una amiga, Carmen.

She has a house in Salamanca.
A hotel costs a lot of money.
Oh, excuse me. One moment, please, it is Carmen.
She is always speaking on the phone.
'Bye!

Tiene una casa en Salamanca.
Un hotel cuesta mucho dinero.
Ah perdón, un momento, por favor, es Carmen.
Siempre habla por teléfono.
¡Hasta luego!

Now say all the sentences in Spanish without stopping and starting.

If you can do it in under one minute you are a fast and fluent winner!

But if you are not happy with your result – just try once more.

Test your progress

This is your only *written* exercise. You'll be amazed at how easy it is! Translate the 20 sentences without looking at the previous pages. The bits in brackets tell you how it is said in Spanish.

1 My name is Peter Smith.
2 Hello, we are Helen and Pepe.
3 I am from Toledo. And you?
4 María is a good friend.
5 I always go home in June.
6 We work in Alicante in August.
7 Do you always go to New York in March?
8 What work do you do? (In what do you work?) Do you work with computers?
9 She is in London with the children.
10 One moment, please. What is it? Does it cost a lot?
11 Does the house have a telephone? No, unfortunately not.
12 Good day. Are you (the) Mrs López from Madrid?
13 I work without pay at an American company.
14 Now I have a better job. I work for three big banks.
15 Paco! How are you? Are we going to Seville?
16 My wife also is American. She is from Boston.
17 We have good seats in the aeroplane.
18 Do I have a Mercedes? Come off it!
19 My girlfriend speaks Spanish (*español*), but not a lot.
20 I am going on holiday with Carmen. Unfortunately she is boring.

When you have finished look up the answers on page 86, and mark your work. Then enter your result on the **Progress chart** on page 9. If your score is higher than 80%, you'll have done very well indeed!

02

week two

35 minutes a day – but a little extra will step up your progress!

25

Day one

- Read **In (the) Sierra Nevada**.
- Listen to/Read **En Sierra Nevada**.
- Listen to/Read the **New words**. Learn 20 easy ones.

Day two

- Repeat **En Sierra Nevada** and the **New words**.
- Go over **Pronunciation**.
- Learn the harder **New words**.
- Use the **Flash words** to help you.

Day three

- Learn all the **New words** until you know them well.
- Read and learn the **Good news grammar**.

Day four

- Cut out and learn the **Flash sentences**.
- Listen to/Read **Learn by heart**.

Day five

- Listen to/Read **Let's speak Spanish**.
- Go over **No tengo mucho dinero, pero**…

Day six

- Listen to/Read **Let's speak more Spanish** (optional).
- Listen to/Read **Let's speak Spanish – fast and fluently** (optional).
- Translate **Test your progress**.

Day seven is a study-free day!

day-by-day guide

In (the) Sierra Nevada

In Malaga Tom and Kate hire a car and drive to the Sierra Nevada. They speak to Rita López of 'Casa Margarita', and later to Paco, the waiter. (*The English of Weeks 1–3 is in 'Spanish-speak' to get you tuned in.*)

Kate Good afternoon. Have you a room double for one night and not very expensive, please?

Rita Yes, I have a room small with bathroom. But the shower is broken. My husband it can repair tomorrow.

Tom Right, where is the room?

Rita Here on the left. Not it is very big.

Kate The room is a little small but nice. How much costs it?

Rita Only €35 but we do not take credit cards. There is a big breakfast from eight to ten and half.

Kate All right, we take the room. But can we take the breakfast at eight less quarter? We would like to go to Marbella tomorrow at eight and quarter.

Rita Agreed.

Kate Can I ask you where we can we take coffee? Is there near here a cafeteria… or a bar? Where are they?

Rita It is very easy. There is a cafeteria at five minutes from here, at some 30 metres on the right and then straight ahead.

(In the cafeteria)

Paco What would you like to take, please?

Kate We would like a coffee with milk and a tea, please.

Paco And something to eat? We have snacks, omelette, toast…

Tom Right… two toasts, please

Tom The table is not clean.

Kate Yes, but the cafeteria is not bad.

Tom My tea is cold.

Kate Yes, but the toilets are great.

Tom The toast is bad.

Kate Yes, but the waiter is very handsome.

Tom I would like the bill, please.

Paco €9.10, please.

▶ En Sierra Nevada

In Malaga Tom and Kate hire a car and drive to the Sierra Nevada.
They speak to Rita López of 'Casa Margarita', and later to Paco, the
waiter.

Kate	Buenas tardes, ¿tiene usted una habitación doble para una noche y no muy cara, por favor?
Rita	Sí, tengo una habitación pequeña con cuarto de baño. Pero la ducha está rota. Mi marido la puede reparar mañana.
Tom	Bueno, ¿dónde está la habitación?
Rita	Aquí, a la izquierda. No es muy grande.
Kate	La habitación es un poco pequeña pero bonita. ¿Cuánto cuesta?
Rita	Sólo treinta y cinco euros, pero no tomamos tarjetas de crédito. Hay un desayuno de ocho a diez y media.
Kate	Vale, tomamos la habitación. Pero, ¿podemos tomar el desayuno a las ocho menos cuarto? Quisiéramos ir a Marbella mañana a las ocho y cuarto.
Rita	De acuerdo.
Kate	¿Puedo preguntarle dónde podemos tomar café? ¿Hay aquí cerca una cafetería… o un bar? ¿Dónde están?
Rita	Es muy fácil. Hay una cafetería a cinco minutos de aquí, a unos treinta metros a la derecha y luego todo recto.

(En la cafetería)

Paco	¿Qué desean tomar, por favor?
Kate	Quisiéramos un café con leche y un té, por favor.
Paco	Y ¿algo para comer? Tenemos tapas, tortilla, tostadas…
Tom	Bueno… dos tostadas por favor.
Tom	La mesa no está limpia.
Kate	Sí, pero la cafetería no es mala.
Tom	Mi té está frío.
Kate	Sí, pero los servicios son estupendos.
Tom	La tostada está mala.
Kate	Sí, pero el camarero es muy guapo.
Tom	Quisiera la cuenta, por favor.
Paco	Nueve euros y diez céntimos, por favor.

▶ New words

una habitación doble *a double room*
una noche *a night*
muy *very*
caro/a *expensive*
pequeño/a *small*
el cuarto de baño *the bathroom*
la ducha *the shower*
roto/a *broken*
el marido *the husband*
lo, la (by itself) *it*
puede *he/she can, you can*
reparar *(to) repair*
mañana *tomorrow*
bueno/a (by itself) *all right, right*
¿dónde? *where?*
aquí *here*
a la izquierda *on the left*
un poco *a little*
bonito/a *pretty, lovely, nice*
¿cuánto? *how much…?*
sólo *only*
treinta y cinco *35*
tomamos *we take*
las tarjetas de crédito *the credit cards*
el desayuno *the breakfast*
hay *there is*
medio *half*
vale *all right, OK*
podemos *we can*
tomar *(to) take*
menos *less*
cuarto *quarter*
quisiera/quisiéramos *I/we would like (to)*
ir *(to) go*
de acuerdo *agreed, OK*

puedo *I can*
preguntar *to ask*
¿puedo preguntarle? *Can I ask you?*
café *coffee*
cerca *near*
una cafetería *a café*
o *or*
están *they are, you are* (plural)
fácil *easy*
minutos *minutes*
unos, unas *some*
treinta metros *thirty metres*
a la derecha *on the right*
luego *then, later*
todo recto *straight ahead*
¿qué desean? *what do you want/wish?*
la leche *the milk*
un té *a tea*
algo *something*
comer *(to) eat*
¿qué tienen ustedes? *What do you have?*
tapas *Spanish snacks*
una tortilla *a Spanish omelette*
tostadas *toast*
la mesa *the table*
limpio/a *clean*
frío/a *cold*
malo/a *bad*
los servicios *the toilets*
son *are, they are*
estupendo/a *marvellous, great*
el camarero *the waiter*
guapo/a *good-looking*
la cuenta *the bill*
el céntimo *cent*

TOTAL NEW WORDS: 70
…only 245 words to go!

▶ Good news grammar

1 *Ser* and *estar*: to be and (not) to be

Unless you are a genius you are bound to get these two mixed up at times. But with **Instant Spanish** everybody will still understand you perfectly. Here are the main differences between **ser** and **estar** which both mean *(to) be*.

You use **ser** when you talk about something which is a basic characteristic of somebody or something and which does not change.
> *My name is Paco*   Mi nombre es Paco. **Soy** Paco.
> *We are English*   **Somos** ingleses.

You also use **ser** for telling the time: ¿Qué hora **es**? **Son** las tres.

You use **estar** when you talk about something that is temporary, that can change.

> Las mesas no **están** limpias. La ducha **está** rota.

You also use **estar** when someone or something is in a place, even if it is permanent!

> **Estamos** en España. Londres **está** en Inglaterra. ¿Dónde **está**? **Está** aquí cerca. **Estoy** en Barcelona.

And if you confuse them?… Don't worry. It's not *that* serious!

Here is a combined verb box. Spend five minutes on it.

ser		estar
soy… Juan	*I am*	estoy… en Madrid
es	*you are*	está
es	*he/she/it is*	está
somos	*we are*	estamos
son	*they are*	están
son	*you are*	están

Remember, *you* and … *you*: use **es** and **está** when you talk to one person. Use **son** and **están** when you talk to two people or more.

2 Saying 'not'

If you want to say in Spanish that you are *not* doing something, you just add **no**. But did you notice what happened to the **no** when Señora López said: 'No es muy grande' and 'No tomamos tarjetas'? The **not** moved in front of the verb. It does this all the time: '...*not* is very big' '...*not* we take credit cards'.

*The table is **not** clean.*   La mesa **no** está limpia.

*I do **not** work.*   **No** trabajo.

No, no trabajo. Don't let this confuse you. The first **no** means *no*, the second one *not*.

3 *Hay*: there is/is there? – there are/are there?

You will use this a lot, especially when asking questions.

¿**Hay** un banco aquí cerca? ¿**Hay** un bar? ¿**Hay** servicios? ¿**Hay** un camarero guapo? ¡Sí, **hay** dos!

4 Telling the time

las siete **menos cuarto**	*quarter to* seven
las diez **y cuarto**	*quarter past* ten
las dos **y media**	*half past* two
la una **y media**	*half past* one

▶ Learn by heart

Learn the six lines **No tengo mucho dinero, pero...** by heart.

When you know them try to say them fluently and fairly fast. How about 45 to 60 seconds?

Choose one of these to fill in the gaps:

mi marido, mi mujer, mi amigo (*boy/male friend*), **mi amiga**

No tengo mucho dinero, pero...

No tengo mucho dinero pero quisiera ir de vacaciones en julio.
Quisiera ir a la Costa del Sol con.. .
Podemos ir a Marbella en el Rover.
No cuesta mucho y la Costa es muy bonita.
¿Podemos ir? ¡No!
Hay siempre mucho trabajo en la empresa y... ¡el Rover está roto!

Once again, give this piece some *life* when you know it by heart. Bits of it will come in handy later!

▶ Let's speak Spanish

Now let's practise what you have learned. Below I give you ten English sentences and you say them in Spanish – OUT LOUD! If you have the recording, listen to check the answers. Tick each sentence if you got it right. Unless you get nine correct, do the exercise again.

1 Do you have a room?
2 It is a little big.
3 At what time is the breakfast?
4 The computers are expensive.
5 We would like to eat something.
6 How much is (costs) the tea?
7 Where is the café? On the right?
8 We are going to Málaga at two.
9 Excuse me, the bill, please.
10 Is there a bank near here?

Now answer the questions on the left with **sí** and speak about yourself, and those on the right with **no** and say 'we'.

11 ¿Tiene una tarjeta Visa?
12 ¿Hay un bar aquí?
13 ¿Es una cuenta muy grande?

14 ¿Están de vacaciones?
15 ¿Trabajan ustedes diez horas?
16 ¿Tienen mucho dinero?

Now think up your own answers. Yours may be different from mine but quite correct.

17 ¿A qué hora va usted a Barcelona?
18 ¿Qué tal las tostadas?
19 ¿Dónde está 'Casa Margarita'?
20 ¿Hay servicios aquí? ¿Y dónde están?

Answers

1 ¿Tiene (usted) una habitación?
2 Es un poco grande.
3 ¿A qué hora es el desayuno?
4 Los ordenadores son caros.
5 Quisiéramos comer algo.
6 ¿Cuánto cuesta el té?
7 ¿Dónde está la cafetería? ¿A la derecha?
8 Vamos a Málaga a las dos.
9 Perdone, la cuenta, por favor.
10 ¿Hay un banco aquí cerca?
11 Sí, tengo una tarjeta Visa.

12 Sí, hay un bar aquí.
13 Sí, es una cuenta muy grande.
14 No, no estamos de vacaciones.
15 No, no trabajamos diez horas.
16 No, no tenemos mucho dinero.
17 Voy a Barcelona a las tres y media.
18 Las tostadas están buenas, pero frías.
19 'Casa Margarita' está en Sierra Nevada.
20 Sí, hay servicios aquí. Están todo recto.

If you managed to get more than half right the first time, give yourself a double gold star!

▶ Let's speak more Spanish

Here are the two optional exercises. Remember, they may stretch the 35 minutes a day by an extra 15 minutes. But the extra practice will be worth it.

In your own words

This exercise will teach you to express yourself freely. Use only the words you have learned so far.

Ask me in your own words…

1 if there is availability of a double room en suite
2 what the price of the room is for one night
3 where you can have a coffee
4 if the café is straight ahead and on the left or on the right

Tell me…

5 you would like breakfast at 7.30
6 you are thinking of driving to Barcelona the next day
7 you want coffee and toast
8 what you don't like about the café
9 what Kate likes about the café (*dice* (she says):…)
10 that the bill is €9.10

Answers

1 ¿Tiene usted una habitación doble con baño o con ducha?
2 ¿Cuánto cuesta la habitación para una noche?
3 ¿Dónde hay una cafetería aquí cerca?
4 La cafetería ¿está todo recto y a la izquierda o a la derecha?
5 Quisiera el desayuno a las siete y media.
6 Quisiera ir a Barcelona mañana.
7 Quisiera café y tostadas.
8 La mesa no está limpia y la tostada está mala.
9 Kate dice: 'Los servicios son estupendos; el camarero es muy guapo.'
10 La cuenta es nueve euros y diez céntimos.

◖ Let's speak Spanish – fast and fluently

No more stuttering and stumbling! Get out the stopwatch and time yourself with this fluency practice.

Translate each section and check if it is correct, then cover up the answers and say the three or four sentences fast!

20 seconds per section for a silver star, 15 seconds for a gold star.

Some of the English is in 'Spanish-speak' to help you.

Good evening, do you have a room with bath?
80 (*ochenta*) euros is a little expensive.
I would like a room with shower.
How much is (costs) the breakfast?

Buenas noches. ¿Tiene usted una habitación con baño?
Ochenta euros es un poco caro.
Quisiera una habitación con ducha.
¿Cuánto cuesta el desayuno?

My company is here very near, straight ahead, on the left.
But I am going tomorrow to Valencia.
I would like to go at 9.30.

Mi empresa está aquí muy cerca, todo recto, a la izquierda.
Pero voy mañana a Valencia.
Quisiera ir a las nueve y media.

The café here is very small and expensive.
The toilets are not clean.
The coffee is cold and there is no tea.
The bill? Two tapas – eight euros.

La cafetería aquí es muy pequeña y cara.
Los servicios no están limpios.
El café está frío y no hay té.
¿La cuenta? Dos tapas – ocho euros.

Now say all the sentences in Spanish without stopping and starting.

If you can do it in under a minute you are a fast and fluent winner!

But if you are not happy with your result – just try once more.

Test your progress

Translate these sentences into Spanish and write them down. See what you can remember without looking at the previous pages.

1 Where is there a telephone? On the right?
2 Can we eat some toast here? Are there seats for four?
3 Do you have a table? At half past eight? We are six.
4 Let's go to the cafeteria, all right?
5 Can you repair the Seat? It is broken.
6 We are in the room. Where are you?
7 The tapas are excellent. I can eat lots.
8 Can I ask you? You have a small company. Is it in Texas?
9 We cannot go on holiday in July. We do not have money.
10 Where is the waiter? Does he have my bill?
11 Where are the toilets? On the left?
12 Maria and I would like to go to Granada – without husbands.
13 Excuse me, I have only €35 and a credit card.
14 €3.10 for a cold tortilla? It is very expensive.
15 I have been in Seville for one night. It costs less in November.
16 Mrs López is very good-looking. Where does she work? Very near?
17 Agreed! We take the Seat for April.
18 London is not pretty in November.
19 I have worked a little with computers. It is not easy.
20 At what time are we going to be here? At one.

Check your answers on page 87 and remember the scoring instructions. Then enter your result on the **Progress chart**.

Another 80% ...?

03

week three

Study for 35 minutes a day – but there are no penalties for doing more!

Day one

- Read **Let's go shopping**.
- Listen to/Read **Vamos de compras**.
- Read the **New words**, then learn some of them.

Day two

- Repeat **Vamos de compras** and the **New words**.
- Learn all the **New words**. Use the **Flash cards!**

Day three

- Test yourself on all the **New words** – Boring, boring, but you are over half way already!
- Listen to/Read **Spot the keys**.
- Learn the **Good news grammar**.

Day four

- Go over the **Good news grammar**.
- Cut out and learn the ten **Flash sentences**.

Day five

- Listen to/Read **Let's speak Spanish**.
- Listen to/Read **Learn by heart**.

Day six

- Go over **Learn by heart**.
- Have a quick look at the **New words** Weeks 1–3. You know 226 words by now! Well, more or less.
- Listen to/Read **Let's speak more Spanish** (optional).
- Listen to/Read **Let's speak Spanish – fast and fluently** (optional).
- Translate **Test your progress**.

Day seven

Enjoy your day off!

day-by-day guide

Let's go shopping

Tom and Kate have rented a holiday apartment just outside Marbella. Kate plans to do some shopping. (*The English of Weeks 1–3 is in 'Spanish-speak' to get you tuned in.*)

Kate   Well, today we must go shopping. Are we going to the (town) centre?

Tom   But it makes bad weather. It makes cold and there is football and tennis in the television... and golf at twelve and half...

Kate   I am sorry but first we must go to a cash dispenser and to a tobacconist or to the post office to buy stamps...and then to the chemist's and the dry cleaner's.

Tom   And so not there is golf... perhaps football at three o'clock... Is that all?

Kate   No, we must go to El Corte Inglés to buy a suitcase new and I have to go to a supermarket and to the hairdresser. And then I would like to buy some shoes.

Tom   Good grief! Until what hour are open the shops?

Kate   I believe (that) until 8 o'clock.

Tom   And so there is not football... perhaps tennis at eight and quarter.

(Later)

Kate   I believe that I have bought too much; a quarter of a kilo of ham, half kilo of cheese, 200 grams of pâté, eggs, bread, butter, sugar, six beers and a bottle of wine red.

Tom   It doesn't matter. There is enough for two days. Not we have eaten anything since yesterday. And what is there in the bag big? Something for me?

Kate   Well, I have gone to the hairdresser of El Corte Inglés and afterwards I have seen some shoes in blue. They are great, aren't they? The sales assistant was very nice and handsome like Tom Cruise.

Tom   Who is Tom Cruise? And how much cost the shoes?

Kate   They were a little expensive... €100... It is the same price in England!

Tom   What? My wife is mad!

Kate   But this T-shirt of golf size 50, was very cheap, only €10, and here I have a newspaper English and is there not now tennis in the television?

▶ Vamos de compras

Tom and Kate have rented a holiday apartment just outside Marbella. Kate plans to do some shopping.

Kate	Pues… hoy tenemos que ir de compras. ¿Vamos al centro?
Tom	Pero hace mal tiempo. Hace frío, y hay fútbol y tenis en la tele… y golf a las doce y media…
Kate	Lo siento, pero primero tenemos que ir a un cajero, y a un estanco o a correos para comprar sellos… y después a la farmacia y a la tintorería.
Tom	Entonces, no hay golf… quizás fútbol a las tres… ¿Es eso todo?
Kate	No, tenemos que ir al Corte Inglés a comprar una maleta nueva, y yo tengo que ir a un supermercado y a la peluquería. Y luego quisiera comprar unos zapatos.
Tom	¡Madre mía! ¿Hasta qué hora están abiertas las tiendas?
Kate	Creo que hasta las ocho.
Tom	Entonces, no hay fútbol… quizás tenis a las ocho y cuarto…

(Más tarde)

Kate	Creo que he comprado demasiado: un cuarto de kilo de jamón, medio kilo de queso, 200 gramos de paté, huevos, pan, mantequilla, azúcar, seis cervezas y una botella de vino tinto.
Tom	No importa. Hay bastante para dos días. No hemos comido nada desde ayer. Y ¿qué hay en la bolsa grande? ¿Algo para mí?
Kate	Pues, he ido a la peluquería del Corte Inglés y después he visto unos zapatos en azul. Son estupendos ¿verdad? El dependiente era muy amable y guapo, como Tom Cruise.
Tom	¿Quién es Tom Cruise? Y ¿cuánto cuestan los zapatos?
Kate	Eran un poco caros… cien euros… ¡Es el mismo precio que en Inglaterra!
Tom	¿Qué? ¡Mi mujer está loca!
Kate	Pero esta camiseta de golf talla 50, era muy barata, sólo diez euros, y aquí tengo un periódico inglés y ¿no hay ahora tenis en la tele?

▶ New words

Learn the new words in half the time by using the **Flash cards**. There are 22 to start you off. Get a friend to make the rest!

hoy *today*
tenemos que *we have to, we must*
ir de compras *go shopping*
al centro *to the centre*
hace mal tiempo *it is bad weather* (lit. it makes…)
hace frío *it is cold* (it makes cold)
el fútbol *the football*
la tele, la televisión *the TV*
lo siento *I'm sorry*
primero *first*
un cajero (automático) *a cash dispenser*
el estanco *the tobacconist*
correos *the post office*
comprar *(to) buy*
los sellos *the stamps*
después *afterwards, then*
la farmacia *the chemist's*
la tintorería *the dry cleaner's*
entonces *and so*
quizás *perhaps*
ese, esa/eso (by itself) *that*
todo *all*
El Corte Inglés *(a Spanish chain of department stores)*
una maleta *suitcase*
nuevo/a *new*
tengo que *I have to, must*
un supermercado *a supermarket*
la peluquería *the hairdresser*
los zapatos *the shoes*
¡Madre mía! *good grief!* (lit. my mother!)
hasta *until*
abierto *open*
la tienda *the shop*
creo *I believe*

que *that, as*
más *more*
más tarde *later*
he comprado *I have bought, I bought*
demasiado *too, too much*
el jamón *the ham*
el queso *the cheese*
un gramo *a gram*
los huevos *the eggs*
el pan *the bread*
la mantequilla *the butter*
el azúcar *the sugar*
la cerveza *the beer*
una botella *a bottle*
el vino tinto *the red wine*
no importa *it doesn't matter, no problem*
bastante *enough, rather*
hemos comido *we have eaten*
nada *nothing*
desde *since*
ayer *yesterday*
la bolsa / el bolso *the bag / the handbag*
para mí *for me*
he ido *I have gone*
he visto *I have seen*
azul *blue*
¿verdad? *isn't it, aren't they, don't you, etc.*
el dependiente *the sales assistant*
era *he/she/it was, I was*
amable *kind, charming*
como *like*
¿quién? *who?*
eran *they were*
el mismo *the same*
el precio *the price*

cien *a hundred*	**la talla** *the size*
Inglaterra *England*	**barato/a** *cheap*
loco/a *crazy*	**un periódico** *a newspaper*
este, esta / esto (by itself) *this*	**inglés** *English*
la camiseta *the T-shirt*	

TOTAL NEW WORDS: 78
...only 167 words to go!

Some easy extras

los colores (the colours)

blanco/a *white*	**amarillo/a** *yellow*
negro/a *black*	**marrón** *brown*
rojo/a *red*	**gris** *grey*
azul *blue*	**naranja** *orange*
verde *green*	**rosa** *pink*

▶ Spot the keys

By now you can say many things in Spanish. But what happens if you ask a question and do not understand the answer? Don't panic and go blank; just listen for the words you know. Any familiar words which you pick up will provide you with key words – clues to what the other person is saying. If you have the recording, close the book now, listen to the dialogue and write down all the key words you have recognized.

Here's an example:

You **Perdone, quisiera ir a correos. ¿Dónde está?**

Answer *Pues, esmuysencillo: siga* **todo recto hasta** *el siguiente cruceconsemáforos. Hay algunosedificios, entreellos* **una casa roja a la izquierda**. *Después hay una residenciadeancianos y* **unas** *cuantas* **tiendas. A la derecha** *hay una* **tintorería**. *Atraviese* **el parking** *y veralaoficina* **de correos**.

With a lot of words running into each other you still managed to pick up: **todo recto – hasta – una casa roja – a la izquierda – unas tiendas – a la derecha – tintorería – el parking – de correos**. I think you'll get there.

▶ Good news grammar

1 The past

Imagine you are getting married today. You would say 'I do.' If it happened yesterday you would say 'I did' or 'I have done it.' When you want to talk about the past in Spanish the easiest way is to use **haber**, another kind of *have* (never **tener**!) plus a changed main verb. For example **trabajar** becomes **trabajado** and **comprar** becomes **comprado**. Let's put it together.

I bought, or I have bought	**he** comprado
You (sing.) bought, or you have bought	**ha** comprado
He/she/it bought, or has bought	**ha** comprado
We bought, or we have bought	**hemos** comprado
They bought, or they have bought	**han** comprado
You (plural) bought, or have bought	**han** comprado

Not all **Instant** verbs are so well behaved and just change to -ado. Here are three odd ones which you'll use all the time.

ir	(*to go*)	but:	**he ido**	*I went, I have gone*
ver	(*to see*)	but:	**he visto**	*I saw, I have seen*
tener	(*to have*)	but:	**he tenido**	*I had, I have had*

If you get confused there's a complete list of all **Instant** verbs in Week 6. Have a sneak preview. You know lots already!

2 *a + el = al*; *de + el = del*

a and **de** plus **el** are always contracted to **al** and **del**.

Vamos **al** centro. Cinco minutos **del** bar.

3 *Tener que*: must, have to

How often do you say *I have to* or *I must*?

Tengo que trabajar. **Tenemos que** comprar... ¿**Tiene que** ir? Don't forget the **que**!

4 *ir* (go) and *poder* (can)

You know the routine. Say **ir** and **poder** with your eyes closed.

	I	*you/he/she/it*	*we*	*they/you*
ir:	voy	va	vamos	van
poder:	puedo	puede	podemos	pueden

▶ Let's speak Spanish

If you have the recording, listen to check your answers. Say them one at a time – OUT LOUD.

1 I am sorry, I have to go.
2 We would like to go shopping.
3 Where are there shops?
4 At what time are they open?
5 I would like to buy bread.
6 Today it is very cold.
7 Good grief! Did you see it?
8 We have to buy beer.
9 We have eaten at (in) El Corte Inglés.
10 You don't have (a) TV? It doesn't matter.

Answer these questions using the 'I' form and the words in brackets.

11 ¿Qué ha comprado? (un periódico inglés)
12 ¿Dónde ha comprado esto? (en el supermercado)
13 ¿Qué ha visto? (muchas tiendas)
14 ¿Qué ha comido? (una paella)
15 ¿Cuántas horas ha trabajado? (ocho horas)

Now answer these questions with **No** and the 'we' form of the verb.

16 ¿Han ido al fútbol?
17 ¿Han comprado la tele?
18 ¿Tienen que ir a correos?
19 ¿Van al centro?
20 Finally, make up a giant sentence without drawing breath using **ahora – centro – Seat – mi amiga – tienda – comprar – zapatos – mi marido**. Start with: **Ahora...**

Answers

1 Lo siento, tengo que ir.
2 Quisiéramos ir de compras.
3 ¿Dónde hay tiendas?
4 ¿A qué hora están abiertas?
5 Quisiera comprar pan.
6 Hoy hace mucho frío.
7 ¡Madre mía! ¿Lo ha visto?
8 Tenemos que comprar cerveza.
9 Hemos comido en El Corte Inglés.
10 ¿No tiene tele? No importa.
11 He comprado un periódico inglés.

12 He comprado esto en el supermercado. *or* Lo he comprado...
13 He visto muchas tiendas.
14 He comido una paella.
15 He trabajado ocho horas.
16 No, no hemos ido al fútbol.
17 No, no hemos comprado la tele.
18 No, no tenemos que ir a correos.
19 No, no vamos al centro.
20 Ahora voy al centro en el Seat con mi amiga a la tienda a comprar zapatos para mi marido.

▶ Let's speak more Spanish

For these optional exercises add an extra 15 minutes to your daily schedule. And remember, don't worry about getting the article or endings wrong. Near enough is good enough!

In your own words

This exercise will teach you to express yourself freely. Use only the words you have learned so far.

Tell me in your own words that...

1 you would like to do the shopping today
2 you are aiming for the middle of the town
3 you are out of cash
4 you have to go first to an ATM...
5 then you have to go to the pharmacy
6 you have seen a shoe shop
7 you have to buy new shoes
8 you bought shoes, and they weren't cheap
9 you did not get much in the supermarket
10 you bought bread and butter, and a little white wine – ten bottles.

Answers

1 Quisiera ir de compras hoy.
2 Voy al centro.
3 No tengo dinero.
4 Primero tengo que ir a un cajero...
5 Después tengo que ir a la farmacia.
6 He visto una tienda de zapatos.
7 Tengo que comprar zapatos nuevos.
8 He comprado zapatos, y no eran baratos.
9 No he comprado mucho en el supermercado.
10 He comprado pan y mantequilla y un poco de vino blanco – diez botellas.

▶ Let's speak Spanish – fast and fluently

Translate each section and check if it is correct, then cover up the answers and say the three or four sentences fast!

20 seconds per section for a silver star, 15 seconds for a gold star.

Some of the English is in 'Spanish-speak' to help you.

Excuse me, are you buying a television?
Is it expensive, the blue television?
No, not too much, in England it is the same price.

¿Perdone, compra usted una tele?
¿Es cara la tele azul?
No, no demasiado, en Inglaterra es el mismo precio.

I would like to buy a suitcase, but not too expensive.
We have a suitcase, but it is too small.
I have seen a suitcase, and it is rather big.

Quisiera comprar una maleta, pero no demasiado cara.
Tenemos una maleta, pero es demasiado pequeña.
He visto una maleta, y es bastante grande.

The weather is very bad in April.
We went to Madrid. We have eaten at (*en*) El Corte Inglés.
Ham, cheese and bread – the bill was 10 euros.
The waiter wasn't handsome but he was very nice.

Hace mal tiempo en abril.
Hemos ido a Madrid. Hemos comido en El Corte Inglés.
Jamón, queso y pan – la cuenta era diez euros.
El camarero no era guapo pero era muy amable.

Now say all the sentences in Spanish without stopping and starting.

If you can do it in under one minute you are a fast and fluent winner!

But if you are not happy with your result – just try once more.

▶ Learn by heart

Try to say this dialogue in under one minute!

Vamos de compras

A Hoy tenemos que ir de compras – vamos al centro.

B Pero hace frío…

A ¡No importa!

B ¡Madre mía! ¡No tengo dinero! ¿Dónde hay un cajero?

A Creo que he comprado demasiado: pan, mantequilla, jamón y queso… y seis botellas de vino blanco.

B ¿Y las cervezas?

A Ah… ¡lo siento!

The more expression you use when saying it, the easier it will be to remember it.

Test your progress

Translate in writing. Then check the answers and be amazed!

1 We can buy stamps at (in) the tobacconist's, can't we?
2 Did you see the tennis on the TV? Yes, I have seen everything.
3 She was very kind, like always.
4 Good grief! The eggs are broken! It doesn't matter.
5 Yesterday was a rather good day.
6 The English newspaper was not cheap.
7 I believe that I have seen a dry cleaner in El Corte Inglés.
8 Until what time do you have to work? Until eight?
9 At what time do we have to go? I cannot go until later.
10 In November it is always bad weather in Manchester.
11 What did you buy? Six bottles of red wine? Great!
12 Size 44: what is that in English? Perhaps 14.
13 It is very cold in this house. I must buy something.
14 First I went shopping and then we ate with friends.
15 We have had the new TV since yesterday. And today it is broken.
16 You have bought a black case, not red, haven't you?
17 Everything was very expensive. So then we did not buy anything.
18 Who is the sales assistant? Where is the milk?
19 We do not have the T-shirt in green and at the same price.
20 I would like to buy something for me. But not too expensive.

Remember to fill in the **Progress chart**. You are now halfway home!

04

week four

Day one

- Read **We're going to eat out**.
- Listen to/Read **Vamos a comer**.
- Read the **New words**. Learn the easy ones.

Day two

- Repeat the dialogue. Learn the harder **New words**.
- Cut out the **Flash words** to help you.

Day three

- Learn all the **New words** until you know them well.
- Read and learn the **Good news grammar**.

Day four

- Cut out and learn the **Flash sentences**.
- Listen to/Read **Learn by heart**.

Day five

- Read **Say it simply**.
- Listen to/Read **Let's speak Spanish**.

Day six

- Listen to/Read **Spot the keys**.
- Listen to/Read **Let's speak more Spanish** (optional).
- Listen to/Read **Let's speak Spanish – fast and fluently** (optional).
- Translate **Test your progress**.

Day seven

Are you keeping your scores above 60%? In that case... **have a good day off!**

day-by-day guide

We're going to eat out

Tom and Kate are still in Marbella. Juan Gálvez invites them to dinner.

Kate Tom, somebody from Madrid has telephoned. He didn't say why (for what). I don't have the number, (it is that) at that moment I didn't have paper. A name like Gámez or Gálvez.

Tom Ah yes, Juan Gálvez, a good client of the company. I know him well. He is very nice. I have an appointment with him on Tuesday. This is for an important matter.

Tom *(On the phone)* Hello, good morning Mr Gálvez. This is Tom Walker... Yes, thank you... yes, sure, that is possible... on Tuesday, next week... correct... that's all right... yes, very interesting... no, we have time... great... no, only some days... oh yes... when?... at nine... upstairs, at the exit... in front of the door. And so, until tonight, thank you very much, until later.

Kate What are we doing this evening?

Tom We are going to eat with Mr Gálvez, in the centre, behind the church. He says that the restaurant is new and very good. He is in Marbella for two days with Edith and Peter Palmer from our company.

Kate I know Edith Palmer. I do not like her. She is boring and very snobbish. She has a terrible dog. I believe that I am going to be ill tonight. A cold with pains. The doctor must come.

Tom No, please! Mr Gálvez is an important client. One cannot do that.

(In the restaurant: Luis explains the menu.)

Luis The fish is not on the menu, and the dessert today is ice cream of the house.

Juan Mrs Walker, what do you like? Perhaps a soup... and afterwards?

Kate Well... a steak with salad, please.

Edith Too much red meat is not good for you.

Juan Mr Walker? Do you like the lamb? And what would you like to drink?

Tom Right... lamb chops for me with chips and vegetables – but all without garlic – and a beer please.

⸺➡ Page 52

▶ Vamos a comer

Tom and Kate are still in Marbella. Juan Gálvez invites them to dinner.

Kate Tom, alguien de Madrid ha llamado. No ha dicho para qué. No tengo el número, es que en ese momento no he tenido papel. Un nombre como Gámez o Gálvez.

Tom Ah, sí, Juan Gálvez, un buen cliente de la empresa. Lo conozco bien. Es muy amable. Tengo una cita con él, el martes. Esto es para una cosa importante.

Tom *(Al teléfono)* Hola, buenos días Señor Gálvez. Soy Tom Walker... Sí, gracias... sí, seguro, eso es posible... el martes, la semana que viene,... correcto... está bien... sí, muy interesante... no, tenemos tiempo... estupendo... no, sólo unos días... ah sí... ¿cuándo?... a las nueve... arriba, a la salida... delante de la puerta... Entonces, hasta esta noche, muchas gracias, hasta luego.

Kate ¿Qué hacemos esta noche?

Tom Vamos a comer con el Señor Gálvez, en el centro, detrás de la iglesia. Dice que el restaurante es nuevo y muy bueno. Está en Marbella durante dos días, con Edith y Peter Palmer de nuestra empresa.

Kate Conozco a Edith Palmer. Ella no me gusta. Es aburrida y muy esnob. Tiene un perro terrible. Creo que esta noche voy a estar enferma. Un resfriado y dolores. El doctor tiene que venir.

Tom ¡No, por favor! El Señor Gálvez es un cliente importante. Eso no se puede hacer.

(En el restaurante: Luis explica el menú.)

Luis El pescado no está en el menú, y el postre hoy es helado de la casa.

Juan Señora Walker, ¿qué le gusta? Quizá una sopa... ¿y después?

Kate Pues... un filete con ensalada, por favor.

Edith Demasiada carne roja no es bueno para usted.

Juan Señor Walker, ¿le gusta el cordero? ¿Y qué quiere usted para beber?

Tom Bueno, para mí chuletas de cordero con patatas fritas y verdura – pero todo sin ajo – y una cerveza, por favor.

······▶ Page 53

Edith	Tom, garlic is very good for you. And I like it very much.
Juan	And you, Mrs Palmer?
Edith	A little roast chicken, a glass of still water, please.

(Later)

Juan	Have we finished? Does anyone want dessert... fruit... a coffee? Nobody? Well then, the bill please.
Edith	Ah, Señor Gálvez, could you help me, please? How do you say 'doggie bag' in Spanish? I would like a bag for my dog.
Kate	But Edith, the dog is in England!

▶ New words

alguien *someone*
ha llamado *has called*
ha dicho *has said*
es que... *it is that, that's because...*
el papel *the paper*
el nombre *the name*
el cliente *the client*
conozco (a) *I know* (usually somebody or a place)
bien *well, all right*
una cita *an appointment*
él *he, him*
martes *Tuesday*
una cosa *a thing, a matter*
importante *important*
gracias, muchas gracias *thank you, thank you very much*
seguro (de) *sure (about)*
posible *possible*
la semana que viene *next week (the week that comes)*
correcto *correct*
interesante *interesting*
tiempo *time,* also: *weather*
arriba *above, upstairs*
la salida *the exit*
delante (de) *in front of*
la puerta *the door*

hacemos *we do*
detrás (de) *behind*
la iglesia *the church*
dice *he/she/it says, you say*
el restaurante *the restaurant*
durante *during, for*
nuestro/a *our*
me gusta/no me gusta *I like (it)/I do not like (it)*
esnob *snobbish*
un perro *a dog*
terrible *terrible*
enfermo *sick, ill*
un resfriado *a cold*
el dolor *the pain*
el doctor *the doctor*
venir *(to) come*
puedo, puede *I can, he/she/it/you can*
no se puede hacer *one cannot do that*
el pescado *the fish*
el menú *the menu*
el postre *the dessert*
helado *ice cream*
le gusta *you like, do you like?*
una sopa *a soup*
un filete *a fillet steak*
una ensalada *a salad*
la carne *the meat*

Edith   Tom, el ajo es muy bueno para usted. Y a mí me gusta mucho.

Juan   ¿Y usted, Señora Palmer?

Edith   Un poco de pollo asado, un vaso de agua sin gas, por favor.

(Más tarde)

Juan   ¿Hemos terminado? ¿Alguien quiere un postre... fruta... un café? ¿Nadie? Bueno, la cuenta, por favor.

Edith   Ah, Señor Gálvez, ¿podría ayudarme, por favor? ¿Cómo se dice 'doggy bag' en español? Quisiera una bolsa para mi perro.

Kate   Pero Edith, ¡el perro está en Inglaterra!

---

el cordero   *the lamb*
¿qué quiere?   *what do you want?*
beber   *(to) drink*
las chuletas   *the chops*
las patatas fritas   *the chips*
la verdura   *the vegetables*
el ajo   *the garlic*
el pollo asado   *the roast chicken*
la fruta   *the fruit*
un vaso   *a glass*

el agua   *the water* (f.)
con/sin gas   *carbonated / non-carbonated*
terminado   *finished*
nadie   *nobody*
¿podría ayudarme?   *could you help me?*
¿cómo...?   *how...?*
¿cómo se dice en español...?   *how does one say in Spanish...?*

> **TOTAL NEW WORDS: 69**
> **...only 98 words to go!**

Some more easy extras

los días de la semana (days of the week)

lunes   *Monday*
martes   *Tuesday*
miércoles   *Wednesday*
jueves   *Thursday*

viernes   *Friday*
sábado   *Saturday*
domingo   *Sunday*

▶ Good news grammar

1 The future

There is an easy way to say something that is going to happen in the future. You don't use *shall* or *will* but simply: *going to* or *go to*.

We are going to buy bread.   **Vamos a comprar pan.**

2 *Me gusta – no me gusta*

I like – I don't like – do you like…? You'll use this a lot! In Spanish **gusta** is a bit of a strange construction. Think of it as saying that **something pleases you**.

me gusta el vino	*I like the wine*
le gusta el Seat	*you like the Seat*
le gusta el pan	*he/she likes the bread*
nos gusta la casa	*we like the house*
les gusta la fruta	*they like the fruit*

If you do not like something simply add **no**:

No me gusta el vino / El vino **no me gusta**. *I do not like the wine*.

When you like or do not like more than one thing use **gustan**:

Las patatas fritas **me gustan mucho. No me gustan** las vacaciones.

3 *Conozco a Edith*   I know Edith

When a verb is followed by a direct object which is a *person* you have to slip in an **a**: **He visto a Pepe** *I have seen Pepe*.

4 *Comer* and *querer*: last two 'gift boxes'

Five minutes each should do it!
Comer is a team player. Many verbs ending in **-er** have endings like him. **Querer** is a rebel. But you'll need **quisiera…** every day.

comer *(to eat)*		querer *(to) wish, want*	
como	I eat	quisiera	I would like
come	you eat	quisiera	you would like
come	he, she, it eats	quisiera	he/she/it would like
comemos	we eat	quisiéramos	we would like
comen	they, you eat	quisieran	they/you would like

▶ 5 Last easy extras: more numbers and time

los números

11	once	19	diecinueve	50	cincuenta
12	doce	20	veinte	60	sesenta
13	trece	21	veintiuno/a	70	setenta
14	catorce	22	veintidós	80	ochenta
15	quince	23	veintitrés	90	noventa
16	dieciséis	30	treinta	100	cien
17	diecisiete	31	treinta y uno/a (etc)	200	doscientos/as
18	dieciocho	40	cuarenta	1,000	mil

¿Qué hora es? (What's the time?)

¿a qué hora?	*at what time?*	**a las cinco**	*at five o'clock*
es la una	*it is one o'clock*	**son las dos**	*it is two o'clock*
un minuto	*a minute*	**una hora**	*an hour*
un día	*a day*	**una semana**	*a week*
un mes	*a month*	**un año**	*a year*

▶ Learn by heart

Here is someone who is rather fed up. Act it out in 45 seconds!

No me gusta...

A ¿Conoce* al Señor Gómez? Es un buen cliente de la empresa. Tengo que ir a comer con él.

B ¿Ah sí?

A No me gusta. No es amable. Come mucho y bebe más.

B ¿Y cuándo?

A ¡Esta noche! Hay fútbol en la tele. Quisiera tener un resfriado pero eso no se puede hacer... ¡Siempre la empresa!

B ¡Lo siento!

*¿Conoce...? *Do you know...?*

Say it simply

When people want to speak Spanish but don't dare, it's usually because they are trying to *translate* what they want to say from English into Spanish. And when they don't know some of the words they give up!

With **Instant Spanish** you work around the words you don't know with the words you do know! Believe me, with 393 words you can say anything! It may not always be very elegant, but you are communicating.

Here are two examples showing you how to say things in a simple way. Words that are not part of the **Instant** vocabulary have been highlighted.

1 You need to **change** your **flight** from Tuesday to Friday.

Saying it simply:

> **No podemos ir el martes, quisieramos ir el viernes.**
> or: **No es posible ir el martes, tenemos que ir el viernes.**

2 You want to get your **purse** from the coach which the driver has locked.

Saying it simply:

> **Lo siento, tengo que ir en el bus. Mi dinero está en el bus.**
> or: **Tengo que tener mi dinero.**
> **Desgraciadamente todo está en el bus.**

Say it simply – in the past

Here are eight essential verbs for when you want to talk about the past – simply.

estar	*to be*	**he estado**	*I was, I have been*
comer	*to eat*	**he comido**	*I ate, I have eaten*
venir	*to come*	**he venido**	*I came, I have come*
hacer	*to do*	**he hecho**	*I did, I have done*
decir	*to say*	**he dicho**	*I said, I have said*
dar	*to give*	**he dado**	*I gave, I have given*
saber	*to know* (a fact)	**he sabido**	*I knew, I have known*
escribir	*to write*	**he escrito**	*I wrote, I have written*

▶ Let's speak Spanish

Here are ten sentences as a warm-up! Use the recording if you have it.

1 I do not like the client.
2 Do we go with him?
3 What do you want, the meat or the fish?
4 Yes, sure, I would like to go home.
5 Do you have an appointment for me?
6 I like going to Mallorca.
7 Who has said that?
8 Has someone called?
9 I know a cheap restaurant.
10 Can you help me, please?

Now pretend you are in Spain with friends who do not speak Spanish. They want you to ask someone things and will want **you** to do it for them in Spanish. They will say: **Please ask him...**

11 if he knows Edith Palmer.
12 if he likes lamb.
13 what he wants to drink.
14 if he has time next week.
15 if he has dogs.

On another occasion they will ask you to **tell** someone things. They say: **Please tell her...** If you don't know the odd word use your **Instant** words.

16 the soup is stone cold.
17 that he/she is a vegetarian.
18 that we are in a rush now.
19 that nobody has seen him.
20 that he/she cannot go tomorrow.

Answers

1 No me gusta el cliente.
2 ¿Vamos con él?
3 ¿Qué quiere, la carne o el pescado?
4 Sí, seguro, quisiera ir a casa.
5 ¿Tiene una cita para mí?
6 Me gusta ir a Mallorca.
7 ¿Quién ha dicho eso?
8 ¿Ha llamado alguien?
9 Conozco un restaurante barato.
10 ¿Puede ayudarme, por favor?
11 ¿Conoce a Edith Palmer?
12 ¿Le gusta el cordero?
13 ¿Qué quiere beber?
14 ¿Tiene tiempo la semana que viene?
15 ¿Tiene perros?
16 Lo siento, pero la sopa está muy fría.
17 Él/Ella no come carne.
18 Lo siento, pero no tenemos tiempo ahora.
19 Nadie lo ha visto.
20 Él/Ella no puede ir mañana.

▶ Let's speak more Spanish

In your own words

This exercise will teach you to express yourself freely. Use only the words you have learned so far.

Tell me in your own words that...

1 somebody has the number of Carlos López
2 you spoke with him on the phone
3 he says he goes to Madrid on Friday
4 he is a very important and good client
5 you believe that you have an appointment with him next week
6 you are going out to eat with Carlos on Saturday
7 Edith Palmer cannot make it – she has a cold
8 you are very fond of tortilla and paella
9 nobody is eating fruit or cheese
10 you went to the restaurant at half past eleven

Answers

1 Alguien tiene el número de Carlos López.
2 He hablado con él por teléfono.
3 Dice que va a Madrid el viernes.
4 Es un cliente muy importante y bueno.
5 Creo que tengo una cita con él la semana que viene.
6 Voy a comer con Carlos el sábado.
7 Edith Palmer no puede ir – tiene un resfriado.
8 Me gustan mucho la tortilla y la paella.
9 Nadie come fruta o queso.
10 He ido al restaurante a las once y media.

▶ Let's speak Spanish – fast and fluently

Translate each section and check if it is correct, then cover up the answers and say the three or four sentences fast!

20 seconds per section for a silver star, 15 seconds for a gold star.

Some of the English is in 'Spanish-speak' to help you.

Do you know Carlos López? He phoned today.
Why? He said it was important.
It was for an appointment on Wednesday.

¿Conoce a Carlos López? Ha llamado hoy.
¿Por qué? Ha dicho que era importante.
Era para una cita el miércoles.

Carlos is only until (the) Friday in Bilbao.
There is a restaurant. It is new, behind the bank.
But I would like to eat with him at my house tonight.

Carlos está en Bilbao sólo hasta el viernes.
Hay un restaurante. Es nuevo, detrás del banco.
Pero quisiera comer con él en mi casa esta noche.

Unfortunately, I cannot go.
My dog is ill. He has pains. He has eaten too much meat.
Oh, I am sorry. How do you say in Spanish: 'Poor little thing?'

Desgraciadamente no puedo ir.
Mi perro está enfermo. Tiene dolores. Ha comido demasiada carne.
Oh, lo siento. ¿Cómo se dice en español: 'Poor little thing'?
('Pobrecito'.)

Now say all the sentences in Spanish without stopping and starting.

If you can do it in under one minute you are a fast and fluent winner!

But if you are not happy with your result – just try once more.

▶ Spot the keys

You practised listening for key words when you asked the way to the post office in Week 3. Now you are in a department store and you ask the sales assistant if the black shoes you liked are also available in size 39:

Perdone, ¿tiene estos zapatos también en número treinta y nueve?

She said **no** then **un momento, por favor** and disappeared. When she came back this is what she said:

Acabo de mirar en el almacén y he llamado a otra sucursal, pero tienen los **zapatos sólo en marrón**. *Pero sé por experiencia que esta marca* **siempre viene en tallas muy grandes** *y en mi opinión el* **número treinta y ocho** *sería* **bastante grande**.

Size 39 was only available in brown but size 38 might be big enough.

Test your progress

1 What did he say? He said: For whom are the chips?
2 Can you come to our house? Next week?
3 She says that the exit of the shop is upstairs behind the bar.
4 Did you say that he has gone to England?
5 What do you want? It is that… I am sick and I cannot work.
6 Could you help me, please? Is there a doctor here?
7 Is he going to the appointment without shoes? One cannot do that.
8 I know Isabel Romero. She is a very interesting woman.
9 Nobody can drink 15 beers in one night. It is not possible.
10 I like (the) dessert very much. I would like the ice cream.
11 He says that it is an important matter, but he has no time.
12 We have finished and now we must go to Valencia.
13 I eat a lot of salads. What do you eat?
14 How do you like the fish? Without garlic?
15 The name of this vegetable: how does one say in Spanish…?
16 There are no shops in front of the church or behind. What do we do?
17 The company called. A Mr López said that it is an important matter.
18 I am sure they have carbonated water. They always have it.
19 He says that he has pains since yesterday. Do you believe it?
20 I have a cold. I cannot go to England today.

How are your 'shares' looking on the **Progress chart**? Going up?

05

week five

How about 15 minutes on the train, tube or bus, ten minutes on the way home and 20 minutes before switching on the television…?

Day one

- Read **On the move**.
- Listen to/Read **De acá para allá**.
- Read the **New words**. Learn 15 or more.

Day two

- Repeat **De acá para allá** and the **New words**.
- Cut out the **Flash words** and get stuck in.

Day three

- Test yourself to perfection on all the **New words**.
- Read and learn the **Good news grammar**.

Day four (the tough day)

- Cut out and learn the **Flash sentences**.
- Listen to/Read **Learn by heart**.

Day five

- Listen to/Read **Let's speak Spanish**.
- Go over **Learn by heart**.

Day six

- Listen to/Read **Spot the keys**.
- Listen to/Read **Let's speak more Spanish** (optional).
- Listen to/Read **Let's speak Spanish – fast and fluently** (optional).
- Translate **Test your progress**.

Day seven

**How is the Progress chart looking? Great?… Great!
I bet you don't want a day off… but I insist!**

day-by-day guide

On the move

Tom and Kate are now travelling through Castilla – by train, bus and hire car. They talk to María, the ticket clerk at the station, to Jim on the train and later to Pepe, the bus driver.

(At the railway station)

Tom　　Two tickets to Toledo, please.

María　Thereandback?

Tom　　There and what? Speak more slowly please.

María　There – and – back?

Tom　　Single, please. When is there a train for Toledo and on what platform?

María　At a quarter to ten, on platform number six.

Kate　　Come on, Tom, there are two seats here in non-smoking. Oh, there is somebody here who smokes. Excuse me, this is for non-smokers. It is forbidden to smoke here.

Jim　　Sorry, I don't understand, I speak only English.

(At the bus stop)

Kate　　They say that the bus for Madrid is coming in about 20 minutes. Tom, please, here are my postcards and a letter. There is a letter-box down there. I am going to take some photos of the river. It is very lovely with the sun.

Tom　　Kate, come on, two buses are coming. The two are yellow. This one is full. Let's take the other one. *(In the bus)* Two to Madrid, please.

Pepe　　This bus goes to Toledo.

Tom　　But we are in Toledo!

Pepe　　Yes, yes, but this bus goes only to the Toledo hospital.

(In the car)

Tom　　Here comes our car. It costs only €40 for three days. I am very pleased.

Kate　　I do not like the car. I believe that it is very cheap because it is very old. Let's hope we do not have problems...

Tom　　I am sorry, but the first car was too expensive, the second one too big, this one was the last.

(Later)

　　　　　The map is not (here). Where is the motorway? On the left there is a petrol station and a stop for the underground and on the right there is a school. Come on!

⸱⸱⸱⸱➡ Page 66

▶ De acá para allá

Tom and Kate are now travelling through Castilla – by train, bus and hire car. They talk to María, the ticket clerk at the station, to Jim on the train and later to Pepe, the bus driver.

(En la estación de ferrocarril)

Tom   Dos billetes para Toledo, por favor.

María   ¿Idayvuelta?

Tom   ¿Ida y qué? Hable más despacio, por favor.

María   ¿Ida – y – vuelta?

Tom   Sólo ida, por favor. ¿Cuándo hay un tren para Toledo y en qué vía?

María   A las diez menos cuarto, en la vía número seis.

Kate   Venga, Tom, hay dos asientos aquí en no fumadores. Oh, aquí hay alguien que fuma. Perdone, esto es para no fumadores. Está prohibido fumar aquí.

Jim   Sorry, no comprendo. Hablo only English.

(En la parada del autobús)

Kate   Dicen que el autobús para Madrid viene en unos veinte minutos. Tom, por favor, aquí están mis tarjetas y una carta. Allí abajo hay un buzón. Yo voy a hacer unas fotos del río. Está muy bonito con el sol.

Tom   Kate, venga, vienen dos autobuses. Los dos son amarillos. Éste está lleno. Vamos a tomar el otro. *(En el autobús)* Dos a Madrid, por favor.

Pepe   Este autobús va a Toledo.

Tom   ¡Pero si estamos en Toledo!

Pepe   Sí, sí, pero este autobús va sólo al hospital de Toledo.

(En el coche)

Tom   Aquí viene nuestro coche. Cuesta sólo cuarenta euros por tres días. Estoy muy contento.

Kate   El coche no me gusta. Creo que es muy barato porque es muy viejo. Espero no tener problemas…

Tom   Lo siento, pero el primer coche era demasiado caro, el segundo demasiado grande, éste era el último.

(Más tarde)

           El mapa no está. ¿Dónde está la autovía? A la izquierda hay una gasolinera y una parada de metro, y a la derecha hay un colegio. ¡Venga!

⸰⸰⸰⸰▶ Page 67

Kate	The main road is over there, (where) the traffic light. If we go to the end of the street we arrive at the motorway. Perhaps some three kilometres. *(On the motorway)* Why does the car go very slowly? Do we have enough petrol? How many litres? Do we have oil? The engine is hot. I believe the car has broken down. Where is the mobile? Where is the number of the garage? Where is my handbag?
Tom	Kate, please, all this is giving me a headache! And here comes the rain. And why are the police driving behind us?

▶ New words

de acá para allá *from here to there, on the move*
la estación *the station*
el ferrocarril *the railway*
el billete *the ticket*
ida y vuelta *return ticket* ('going and returning')
hable *speak*
más despacio *more slowly*
¿cuándo? *when?*
el tren *the train*
la vía *the platform*
venga *come!, come on!*
no fumadores *non-smoking*
fuma *he/she/it smokes, you smoke*
prohibido *forbidden*
fumar *(to) smoke*
comprendo *I understand*
hablo *I speak*
la parada *the stop*
el autobús *the bus*
dicen *they say*
viene *he/she/it comes, you come*
las tarjetas *the postcards*
la carta *the letter*
abajo *below, downstairs*
el buzón *the letter-box*

hacer *do, make*
la foto *the photo*
el río *the river*
el sol *the sun*
vienen *they come*
éste *this one*
lleno *full*
el otro, la otra *the other*
si *if*
el hospital *the hospital*
el coche *the car*
por *for*
contento/a *pleased*
porque *because*
viejo/a *old*
espero *I hope*
el problema *the problem*
segundo/a *second*
último/a *last*
el mapa *the map*
la autovía *the motorway*
la gasolinera *the petrol station*
el metro *the underground*
un colegio *a school, college*
la carretera *the main road*
el semáforo *the traffic light*
el final *the end*
la calle *the street*
llegamos *we arrive*

Kate	La carretera está allí, donde el semáforo. Si vamos hasta el final de la calle llegamos a la autovía. Quizás unos tres kilómetros. *(En la autovía)* ¿Por qué va el coche muy lento? ¿Tenemos suficiente gasolina? ¿Cuántos litros? ¿Tenemos aceite? El motor está caliente. Creo que el coche está roto. ¿Dónde está el movil? ¿Dónde está el número del taller? ¿Dónde está mi bolso?
Tom	Kate, por favor, todo esto me da dolor de cabeza. ¡Y aquí viene la lluvia! ¿Y por qué va la policía detrás de nosotros?

el kilómetro   *the kilometre*
¿por qué?   *why?*
lento/a   *slow*
suficiente   *enough*
la gasolina   *the petrol*
el litro   *the litre*
el aceite   *the oil*
el motor   *the motor*

caliente   *hot*
el taller   *repair garage*
me   *me*
da   *he/she/it gives, you give*
el dolor de cabeza   *the headache*
la lluvia   *the rain*
la policía   *the police*

TOTAL NEW WORDS: 69
…only 29 words to go!

Good news grammar

1 *lo* and *la*: it – *los* and *las*: them

If you want to refer to something or someone – **el camarero, la
cuenta, los servicios** or **las tortillas** – in English, you would say
it or *them*. In Spanish you use **lo** (for **el** words), **la, los** or **las**.
Tengo el coche. *I have it.* **Lo tengo. Tengo la cuenta.** *I have it.*
La tengo! Easy! The **lo, la, los** or **las** always go *in front of* the
first verb:

> Mi marido **la** (la ducha) puede reparar. *My husband it can
> repair.*

2 *¿por qué?... porque...* (twins, but not identical)

por qué means *why?* Think of it as 'for what?'
porque means *because.* Think of it as 'for that...'

3 *¿qué?... que...* (more twins, not identical)

Have you noticed that all the question words carry accents?

> **¿cuándo? ¿cuánto? ¿cómo? ¿dónde? ¿qué?**

Some of these reappear without the accent to introduce the
answer.

> **¿Cómo es Bombay? Como Nueva York.** *Like New York.*

4 Pronouns: *me, mí, le, lo, la, él, ella, nos, les, los, las, ellos, ellas...* and more

Learning these 'cold' is rather disagreeable. Pick them up from
the stories or from the **Flash sentences**. It's easier that way.

▶ Learn by heart

Someone has crashed the car and someone else is getting
suspicious... Say these lines like a prize-winning play!

Vamos al tenis

A ¿Vamos al tenis? Tengo dos billetes de la empresa. Me
gustan mucho los americanos. Vamos en autobús o quizás en
el metro. Hay también un tren, todo el día.

B ¿El autobús, el metro, un tren? ¿Por qué? Hay algo que no me
gusta. Tenemos un coche abajo en la calle.

A Pues... con la lluvia no he visto el semáforo. Pero no es
mucho, sólo la puerta, ¡y el jefe* del taller era muy amable!

*el jefe: *the boss*

▶ Let's speak Spanish

Here's your ten-point warm up: respond to the answers with a question, referring to the words in CAPITAL LETTERS.

Example PEDRO está aquí. ¿QUIÉN está aquí?

1 El móvil no está EN MI BOLSO.
2 LA AUTOVÍA está al final de la carretera.
3 Hay un autobús EN VEINTE MINUTOS.
4 MI MARIDO quisiera hablar con el Señor González.
5 Ida y vuelta a Madrid cuesta QUINCE EUROS.
6 La casa no me gusta PORQUE ES VIEJA.
7 Van a Inglaterra EN COCHE.
8 Habla inglés MUY LENTO.
9 NO, el sueldo no me gusta.
10 SÍ, he estado contenta en el colegio.

While out shopping with a friend you are offered various items to buy. You'll take them all saying: 'Yes, we'll buy it' or 'Yes, we'll buy them'.

11 ¿...y la cerveza?
12 ¿...y el periódico?
13 ¿...y los pollos?
14 ¿...y las camisetas?
15 ¿...y el Mercedes?
16 ¿...y mi casa?

Here are four things you want to refer to but you don't know how to say them in Spanish. Explain them using the words you do know.

17 an au pair
18 kennels
19 a teacher
20 to be broke

Answers

1 ¿Dónde está el móvil?
2 ¿Qué está al final de la carretera?
3 ¿Cuándo hay un autobús?
4 ¿Quién quisiera hablar con el Señor González?
5 ¿Cuánto cuesta a Madrid ida y vuelta?
6 ¿Por qué no le gusta la casa?
7 ¿En qué van a Inglaterra?
8 ¿Cómo habla inglés?
9 ¿Le gusta el sueldo?
10 ¿Ha estado contenta en el colegio?
11 Sí, la compramos.
12 Sí, lo compramos.
13 Sí, los compramos.
14 Sí, las compramos.
15 ¡Sí, lo compramos!
16 ¡Sí, la compramos!
17 Una señora que ayuda con el trabajo en la casa.
18 Una casa para los perros cuando estamos de vacaciones.
19 Una señora o un señor que trabaja con los niños en el colegio.
20 No tenemos dinero.

▶ Let's speak more Spanish

In your own words

This exercise will teach you to express yourself freely. Use only the words you have learned so far.

Tell me in your own words that...

1 you bought a return ticket to Almería
2 you believe there is a train at 10.15
3 you have a seat in non-smoking
4 on Monday you wouldn't mind going by bus to Toledo
5 you must take some photos for your company.
6 this bus is 'chock-a-block'; you are going to take the other one
7 your car is coming on Thursday; it is new but very cheap
8 your wife says 'It's terrible, I don't like it'
9 she says the car is too slow and the engine always overheats
10 hopefully you won't have problems

Answers

1 He comprado un billete de ida y vuelta para Almería.
2 Creo que hay un tren a las diez y cuarto.
3 Tengo un asiento en no fumadores.
4 El lunes quisiera ir a Toledo en autobús.
5 Tengo que tomar unas fotos para mi empresa.
6 Este autobús está lleno. Voy a tomar el otro.
7 Mi coche viene el jueves. Es nuevo pero muy barato.
8 Mi mujer dice: 'Es terrible, no me gusta.'
9 Dice que el coche es demasiado lento y el motor está siempre muy caliente.
10 Espero no tener problemas.

► Let's speak Spanish – fast and fluently

Translate each section and check if it is correct, then cover up the answers and say the three or four sentences fast!

25 seconds per section for a silver star, 20 seconds for a gold star.

Some of the English is in 'Spanish-speak' to help you.

A ticket to Madrid, please. Only one way.
How much? I am sorry, please speak more slowly.
Yes, I would like a seat in smoking.

Un billete para Madrid por favor, sólo ida.
¿Cuánto? Lo siento, hable más despacio, por favor.
Sí, quisiera un asiento en fumadores.

My wife is going to take a photo of the post box.
In Spain the post boxes are yellow, not red like in England.
Unfortunately, it is full.
What are we going to do with the letters?

Mi mujer va a tomar una foto del buzón.
En España, los buzones son amarillos, no rojos como en Inglaterra.
Desgraciadamente, está lleno.
¿Qué hacemos con las cartas?

We don't have a map of Andalucía.
I can't see the road to the motorway.
All the traffic lights are (in) red.
My wife has a headache.
Oh dear.

No tenemos un mapa de Andalucía.
No puedo ver la carretera a la autovía.
Todos los semáforos están en rojo.
Mi mujer tiene dolor de cabeza.
¡Madre mía!

Now say all the sentences in Spanish without stopping and starting.

If you can do it in under one minute you are a fast and fluent winner!

But if you are not happy with your result – just try once more.

▶ Spot the keys

This time you plan a trip in the country and wonder about the weather. This is what you would ask:

You   **Perdone, ¿sabe qué tiempo tenemos hoy?**

Answer   *Pues,* **no estoy** *muy* **segura, pero** *de acuerdo con la última previsión* **en la tele** *hay un sistema lento de bajas presiones que se está alejando hacia el norte y se espera que* **hoy** *el* **tiempo** *sea bastante* **caliente,** *es decir unos* **treinta** *grados, pero por la* **noche** *se espera algunas tormentas y* **lluvia.**

She isn't sure, but according to the TV, something slow is happening (?) and it will be warm tomorrow – 30°C – but something (?) and rain in the night.

Test your progress

Translate into Spanish.

1   I don't like this car. The other car was better.
2   How much does the ticket cost – one way only?
3   What did you say? Speak more slowly, please.
4   We hope to buy petrol cheaper (more cheap) in Spain.
5   It is forbidden to smoke in the underground.
6   Is this correct? A yellow letter-box? I did not know it.
7   Can I speak with the mechanic? We are (at) 30 km from Madrid.
8   What is slower: the train or the car on (in) the motorway?
9   He did not see the traffic light, and now they are in the hospital.
10 There is a chemist's on (in) the main road, at (in) the bus stop.
11 I would like two return tickets, non-smoking.
12 The problem with her is that she smokes too much.
13 He has come here, to the end of the platform.
14 There is a lot of rain in England. I am pleased to be in Spain.
15 They say that the river is five minutes from the station.
16 If he does not give me the money, I am going to the police.
17 This is the last petrol station. Do we have enough oil and water?
18 They come in July. I do not understand why Pedro comes later.
19 I speak with him now. I have a mobile.
20 He has not eaten anything because he has (a) headache.

If you know all your words you should score over 90%!

06

week six

This is your last week! Need I say more?

Day one

- Read **In the airport**.
- Listen to/Read **En el aeropuerto**.
- Read the **New words**. There are only 29!

Day two

- Repeat **En el aeropuerto.** Learn all the **New words**.
- Work with the **Flash words** and **Flash sentences**.

Day three

- Test yourself on the **Flash sentences**.
- Listen to/Read and learn **¡Adiós!**

Day four

- No more **Good news grammar!** Have a look at the summary.
- Read **Say it simply**.

Day five

- Listen to/Read **Spot the keys**.
- Listen to/Read **Let's speak Spanish**.

Day six

- Listen to/Read **Let's speak more Spanish** (optional).
- Listen to/Read **Let's speak Spanish – fast and fluently** (optional).
- Your last **Test your progress!** Go for it!

Day seven

Congratulations!

**You have successfully completed the course
and can now speak**

Instant Spanish!

In the airport

Tom and Kate are on their way home to Birmingham. They are in the departure lounge of Barcelona airport and meet an old friend...

Tom   We have to work on Monday. What a bore! I would like to go to Italy, or better, to Hawaii. My company can wait and nobody is going to know where I am.

Kate   And what are the people in *my* company going to say? They are going to wait for two days and then they are going to phone my mother. She certainly knows the number of my mobile. And then?

Tom   Yes, yes, I know it. Well, perhaps a week's holiday at Christmas in the snow or on a boat to Madeira... I am going to buy a newspaper... Kate! Here is Pedro Iglesias!

Pedro   Well, hello! How are you? What are you doing here? This is my wife, Nancy. How were your holidays? Are they finished?

Kate   The holidays...? hmmm... great! Now we know Andalucia and Castilla well.

Pedro   Next year you must go to Santander or Pamplona. Mrs Walker, my wife would like to buy a book about computers. Would you mind going with her and helping her, please? Mr Walker, you have a newspaper. What is happening with the football? And... would you like to have a drink?

(In a shop at the airport)

Kate   I don't see anything. There is nothing that I like. Are you also going to England?

Nancy   No, we are going to Madrid to (the house of) Pedro's mother. Our children are always there during the holidays. We have one son and three daughters. Tomorrow we are going to take the train. It is cheaper.

Kate   Your husband works for the Bank of Spain, doesn't he?

Nancy   Yes, his work is interesting but the pay is bad. We have a small apartment and an old car. We have to repair lots of things. My mother is in Los Angeles and I have a girlfriend in Dallas and we write (to us) a lot of e-mails. I would like to go to America but it costs too much money.

··········➡ Page 78

▶ En el aeropuerto

Tom and Kate are on their way home to Birmingham. They are in the departure lounge of Barcelona airport and meet an old friend...

Tom   El lunes tenemos que trabajar. ¡Qué lata! Quisiera ir a Italia o mejor a Hawaii. Mi empresa puede esperar, y nadie va a saber dónde estoy.

Kate   ¿Y qué va a decir la gente en *mi* empresa? Van a esperar durante dos días y después van a llamar a mi madre. Seguro que ella sabe el número de mi móvil. ¿Y después?

Tom   Sí, sí, lo sé. Pues, quizás en Navidad una semana de vacaciones en la nieve o en barco a Madeira... Voy a comprar el periódico... ¡Kate! ¡Aquí está Pedro Iglesias!

Pedro   ¡Hombre! ¿Qué tal?¿Qué hacen aquí? Ésta es mi mujer, Nancy. ¿Qué tal las vacaciones, han terminado?

Kate   ¿Las vacaciones...? hmmm... ¡estupendas! Ahora conocemos bien Andalucía y Castilla.

Pedro   El año que viene tienen que ir a Santander o Pamplona. Señora Walker, mi mujer quisiera comprar un libro de ordenadores. ¿Le importaría ir con ella y ayudarla, por favor? Señor Walker, usted tiene un periódico. ¿Qué pasa con el fútbol? Y... ¿quiere tomar una copa?

(En una tienda del aeropuerto)

Kate   No veo nada. No hay nada que me gusta. ¿Va usted también a Inglaterra?

Nancy   No, vamos a Madrid a casa de la madre de Pedro. Nuestros niños siempre están allí durante las vacaciones. Tenemos un hijo y tres hijas. Mañana vamos a tomar el tren. Es más barato.

Kate   Su marido trabaja en el Banco de España, ¿verdad?

Nancy   Sí, su trabajo es interesante, pero el sueldo es malo. Tenemos un piso pequeño y un coche viejo. Tenemos que reparar muchas cosas. Mi madre está en Los Ángeles y tengo una amiga en Dallas y nos escribimos muchos correos electrónicos. Quisiera ir a América pero cuesta demasiado dinero.

Kate	But you have a lovely house in Mallorca.
Nancy	A house in Mallorca? I have never been in Mallorca. When we have holidays we go to (the house of) a friend in Bilbao.
Tom	Kate, come on, we have to go to the plane. Goodbye…! What is the matter, Kate? What did Nancy say?
Kate	Wait Tom, wait…!

▶ New words

el aeropuerto   *the airport*

¡qué lata!   *what a bore, nuisance!*

esperar   *(to) wait*

saber   *(to) know* (a fact)

decir   *(to) say*

la gente   *the people*

llamar (por teléfono)   *(to) call (on the phone)*

la madre   *the mother*

sé   *I know*

en Navidad   *at Christmas*

la nieve   *the snow*

el barco   *the ship, boat*

¡hombre!   *well, hello!* (surprise greeting)

hacen   *they do, you do*

conocemos   *we know*

el libro   *the book*

¿Le importaría?   *would you mind?*

¿qué pasa?   *what is happening? what is the matter?*

una copa   *a drink*

veo   *I see*

el hijo   *the son, child* (m)

la hija   *the daughter, child* (f)

el piso   *the apartment, flat*

vive   *he/she/it lives, you live*

nos   *us*

escribimos   *we write*

el correo electrónico   *the e-mail*

espera / espere   *wait* (friendly) / (formal)

nunca   *never*

TOTAL NEW WORDS: 29
TOTAL SPANISH WORDS LEARNED: 393
EXTRA WORDS: 78

GRAND TOTAL: 471

Kate	Pero usted tiene una casa bonita en Mallorca.
Nancy	¿Una casa en Mallorca? No he estado nunca en Mallorca. Cuando tenemos vacaciones vamos a la casa de un amigo en Bilbao.
Tom	Kate, venga, tenemos que ir al avión. ¡Adiós...! ¿Qué pasa, Kate? ¿Qué ha dicho Nancy?
Kate	¡Espera, Tom, espera...!

▶ Learn by heart

This is your last dialogue to learn by heart. Give it your best! You now have six prize-winning party pieces, and a large store of everyday sayings which will be very useful.

¡Adiós...!

Kate Señor Gálvez, buenos días, soy Kate Walker.
Llamo del aeropuerto.
Sí, las vacaciones han terminado y el dinero también, desgraciadamente.
Tom quisiera hablar con usted...y...¡adiós!

Tom ¡Hola, Juan! ¿Qué? ¿Cómo? ¿Compra los dos?
¿Mi empresa tiene su correo electrónico? ¡Estupendo!
¡Muchas gracias!
¿El año que viene?
Kate quisiera ir a Italia, pero a mí me gusta España.
¿Con Edith Palmer? **¡Por favor!**
Tenemos que ir al avión... ¡Adiós!

Good news grammar

As promised there is no new grammar in this lesson, just a summary of all the 31 **Instant** verbs which appear in the six weeks. This is not for learning, just for a quick check. You know and have used most of them!

Basic form	I	You, he, she, it	We	They, you	The past: haber + ...
ayudar*	ayudo	ayuda	ayudamos	ayudan	ayudado
beber*	bebo	bebe	bebemos	beben	bebido
comer*	como	come	comemos	comen	comido
comprar*	compro	compra	compramos	compran	comprado
comprender*	comprendo	comprende	comprendemos	comprenden	comprendido
conocer	conozco	conoce	conocemos	conocen	conocido
creer*	creo	cree	creemos	creen	creido
costar		cuesta		cuestan	
dar	doy	da	damos	dan	dado
decir	digo	dice	decimos	dicen	dicho
escribir	escribo	escribe	escribimos	escriben	escrito
esperar*	espero	espera	esperamos	esperan	esperado
estar	estoy	está	estamos	están	estado
fumar*	fumo	fuma	fumamos	fuman	fumado
haber	he	ha	hemos	han	
hablar*	hablo	habla	hablamos	hablan	hablado
hacer	hago	hace	hacemos	hacen	hecho
ir	voy	va	vamos	van	ido
llamar*	llamo	llama	llamamos	llaman	llamado
llegar*	llego	llega	llegamos	llegan	llegado
poder	puedo	puede	podemos	pueden	podido
querer	quisiera	quisiera	quisiéramos	quisieran	
reparar*	reparo	repara	reparamos	reparan	reparado
saber	sé	sabe	sabemos	saben	sabido
ser	soy	es	somos	son	sido
tener	tengo	tiene	tenemos	tienen	tenido
tomar*	tomo	toma	tomamos	toman	tomado
trabajar*	trabajo	trabaja	trabajamos	trabajan	trabajado
venir	vengo	viene	venimos	vienen	venido
ver	veo	ve	vemos	ven	visto
vivir	vivo	vive	vivimos	viven	vivido

*member of the Good Verbs Team (see page 17)

Say it simply

Here are two more exercises to practise using plain language:

1 You have just hired a car and notice a big scratch on the left, behind the door. You want to report it so as not to get the bill for it later.

2 You are Kate Walker at the airport, about to catch your flight home when you realize that you have left some clothes behind in the room of your hotel. You phone the hotel to ask the housekeeper to send the things on to you.

What would you say? Say it, then write it down. Then see page 90.

▶ Spot the keys

Here are two final practice rounds. If you have the recording, close the book now. Find the key words and try to get the gist of it. Then check on page 90.

1 This is what you might ask of a taxi driver:

You   ¿En cuánto tiempo se llega* al aeropuerto y cuánto cuesta?

Answer   *Depende de la hora en que vaya a salir. Normalmente se llega en unos veinte minutos, pero si viajamos en hora punta y hay mucho tráfico y si hay atascos sobre el puente del río debe calcular unos cuarenta y cinco minutos. El precio se indica en el taxímetro. Normalmente cuesta entre veinte y veinticinco euros.*

(*in how much time does one arrive = how long does it take)

2 While killing time in the departure lounge of the airport you can't help listening to someone who seems to be raving about something. Identify keys and guess where they have been. The answer is on page 90.

...y mi marido dijo también que le había gustado mucho más que nuestras vacaciones aquí. Y la gente era muy amable y no tan reservada como siempre dicen. Y el hotel estaba directamente sobre el lago, con unas habitaciones muy bonitas y hacía un tiempo estupendo y paseámos muchísimo y también fuimos de excursión con el coche y vimos tantas cosas interesantes. Y entonces decidimos sin más que el año que viene vamos a volver...

► Let's speak Spanish

Here's a five-point warm up: answer these questions using the words in brackets.

1 ¿Ha comprado el piso en Marbella? (Sí, lo, lunes)
2 ¿Cuántos años ha trabajado allí? (durante tres)
3 ¿Cuándo ha hablado con la empresa? (con ella, esta semana)
4 ¿Por qué tiene que reparar su coche? (mi coche, porque es viejo)
5 ¿Ha ido primero con su madre? (no, con el cliente)

In your last exercise you are going to interpret again, this time telling your Spanish friend what others have said in English. Each time say the whole sentence OUT LOUD, translating the English words.

6 Alguien ha dicho que está loco (*if you buy this old flat*).
7 Alguien ha dicho que no le gusta (*if we eat too late*).
8 Ha dicho que algo está roto (*if you have no hot water*).
9 Mi amiga ha dicho (*that our holidays are over*).
10 Ha dicho también (*that next year we go to America*).
11 Mi mujer quisiera decir (*that she has a cold*).
12 Mi marido dice que no puede venir (*because he works on a ship*).
13 No puede venir en Navidad (*because his friend is coming*).
14 Mi amigo dice (*that you are very good-looking*).
15 También dice (*that he would like your* (su) *mobile number*).

Answers

1 Sí, lo he comprado el lunes.
2 He trabajado allí durante tres años.
3 He hablado con ella esta semana.
4 Tengo que reparar mi coche porque es viejo.
5 No, primero he ido con el cliente.
6 ...si compra este piso viejo.
7 ...si comemos demasiado tarde.
8 ...si no tiene agua caliente.
9 ...que nuestras vacaciones han terminado.
10 ...que el año que viene vamos a América.
11 ...que tiene un resfriado.
12 ...porque trabaja en un barco.
13 ...porque viene su amigo.
14 ...que usted es muy guapo/a.
15 ...que quisiera su número móvil.

Now do it once more – **FAST!**

► Let's speak more Spanish

In your own words

This exercise will teach you to express yourself freely. Use only the words you have learned so far.

Tell me in your own words that...

1 next week you have to work
2 you don't like it; you'd rather have more leave
3 nobody knows that you are in Italy
4 your mother has the number of your mobile phone
5 your vacation in Spain was wonderful
6 you did a lot of sightseeing and overeating
7 your friend Mr López is on his way to Granada today
8 he is catching a train to Seville tomorrow
9 you and your wife must fly to America, because your father is ill.
10 you would like to go to Africa for Christmas, but by boat.

Answers

1 La semana que viene tengo que trabajar.
2 No me gusta. Quisiera tener más vacaciones.
3 Nadie sabe que estoy en Italia.
4 Mi madre tiene el número de mi móvil.
5 Las vacaciones en España eran estupendas.
6 He visto mucho y he comido más.
7 Mi amigo, el señor López, va hoy a Granada.
8 Va a tomar el tren para Sevilla mañana.
9 Mi mujer y yo tenemos que ir a América porque mi padre está enfermo.
10 Quisiera ir a África en Navidad, pero en barco.

▶ Let's speak Spanish – fast and fluently

Translate each section and check if it is correct, then cover up the answers and say the three or four sentences fast!

30 seconds for a silver star, 20 seconds for a gold star.

The people in my company do not work a lot.
They write many letters on the computer and always talk on the mobile phone.

La gente en mi empresa no trabaja mucho.
Escriben muchas cartas en el ordenador y siempre hablan por el móvil.

I know Andalucía and Castilla very well.
Next year I would like to see Santander.
I must buy a book of the Paradors of Spain.

Conozco muy bien Andalucía y Castilla.
Quisiera ver Santander el año que viene.
Tengo que comprar un libro de los paradores de España.

Well, hello, what are you doing here? What's the matter?
I need to repair my car and my flat. Both (the two) are very old.
The bill is terrible. Can you help me please – with 200 euros?

Hombre, ¿qué hace aquí? ¿Qué pasa?
Tengo que reparar mi coche y mi piso. Los dos son muy viejos.
La cuenta es terrible. ¿Puede ayudarme, por favor – con doscientos euros?

Now say all the sentences in Spanish without stopping and starting.

If you can do it in under one minute you are a fast and fluent winner!

But if you are not happy with your result – just try once more.

Test your progress

A lot has been crammed into this last test – all 31 **Instant** verbs! But don't panic – it looks worse than it is. Go for it – you'll do brilliantly!

Translate into Spanish.

1   I like writing letters because I have a new computer.
2   How are you? What is the matter? Can I help you?
3   The people in the company are (is) rather boring.
4   I do not have the number of her mobile, I am sorry.
5   Do you like the Sierra Nevada? We had a lot of snow this year.
6   The second case is in the bus. Did you see the black bag?
7   How many cards did you write (at) (in) Christmas? Eighty-eight?
8   That's terrible. They have not eaten for five days.
9   Why did you not telephone? We waited since yesterday.
10 When we arrive we'll have (we take) a drink – or two.
11 Don't you know that? The airport is always open – day and night.
12 We are sure that he has done it.
13 We have worked (for) many years but never on a boat.
14 I have given my car to my son. He is very pleased.
15 Your mother is very nice and makes great paella.
16 Do you live in a house or a flat in Torremolinos?
17 We must work many hours. Four daughters cost a lot of money.
18 Can the garage repair that? I hope so.
19 I know him. He always goes shopping with his dog.
20 Who said one cannot smoke here?
21 We go by plane to Dallas. Then we go by car to Las Vegas.
22 I would like to speak with the sales assistant. He did not give me the bill.
23 We drank your wine but we have come today with two more bottles.
24 I am sorry, but **Instant Spanish** is now finished.

Check your answers on page 89. Then enter a final excellent score on the **Progress chart** and write out your **Certificate!**

answers

How to score

From a total of 100%
- Subtract 1% for each wrong or missing word.
- Subtract 1% for the wrong form of the verb. Example *we have* **tengo (tenemos)**.
- Subtract 1% every time you mix up the present and the past tenses.

There are no penalties for:
- wrong use of all those little words, like: **el/la**, **un/una**, etc.
- wrong ending of adjectives like: **un coche barata (barato)**.
- wrong use of **ser** and **estar**
- wrong choice of words with similar meaning like **en** and **a**
- wrong or different word order
- wrong spelling or missing accents – as long as you can *say* the word: **qué/que**, **quatro (cuatro)**, **ora (hora)**, **rotto (roto)**, etc.
- missing or incorrect punctuation like ¿ or ¡.

100% LESS YOUR PENALTIES WILL GIVE YOU YOUR WEEKLY SCORE

▶ Week 1: Test your progress

1 Me llamo Peter Smith.
2 ¡Hola, somos Helen y Pepe!
3 Soy de Toledo. ¿Y usted?
4 María es una buena amiga.
5 Siempre voy a casa en junio.
6 Trabajamos en Alicante en agosto.
7 ¿(Usted) Va siempre a Nueva York en marzo?
8 ¿En qué trabaja (usted)? ¿Trabaja (usted) con ordenadores?
9 Está en Londres con los niños.
10 Un momento por favor. ¿Qué es? ¿Cuesta mucho?

11 ¿La casa tiene teléfono? No, desgraciadamente, no.
12 Buenos días. ¿Es usted la señora López de Madrid?
13 Trabajo sin sueldo en una empresa americana.
14 Ahora tengo un trabajo mejor. Trabajo para tres bancos grandes.
15 ¡Paco! ¿Qué tal? ¿Vamos a Sevilla?
16 Mi mujer también es americana. Es de Boston.
17 Tenemos buenos asientos en el avión.
18 ¿Yo tengo un Mercedes? ¡Qué va!
19 Mi amiga habla español, pero no mucho.
20 Voy de vacaciones con Carmen. Desgraciadamente es aburrida.

```
YOUR SCORE: ___ %
```

Correct those answers which differ from ours. Then read them out loud twice.

▶ Week 2: Test your progress

1 ¿Dónde hay un teléfono? ¿A la derecha?
2 ¿Podemos comer unas tostadas aquí? ¿Hay asientos para cuatro?
3 ¿Tiene una mesa? ¿A las ocho y media? Somos seis.
4 Vamos a la cafetería, ¿vale?
5 ¿Puede reparar el Seat? Está roto.
6 Estamos en la habitación. ¿Dónde está (usted)?
7 Las tapas están estupendas. Puedo comer muchas.
8 ¿Puedo preguntarle? (Usted) Tiene una empresa pequeña. ¿Está en Texas?
9 No podemos ir de vacaciones en julio. No tenemos dinero.
10 ¿Dónde está el camarero? ¿Tiene mi cuenta?
11 ¿Dónde están los servicios? ¿A la izquierda?
12 María y yo quisiéramos ir a Granada – sin maridos.
13 Perdone, tengo sólo treinta y cinco euros y una tarjeta de crédito.
14 ¿Tres euros y diez céntimos para una tortilla fría? Es muy cara.
15 He estado en Sevilla para una noche. Cuesta menos en noviembre.
16 La Señora López es muy guapa. ¿Dónde trabaja? ¿Muy cerca?
17 ¡De acuerdo! Tomamos el Seat para abril.
18 Londres no es bonito en noviembre.
19 He trabajado un poco con ordenadores. No es fácil.
20 ¿A qué hora vamos a estar aquí? A la una.

```
YOUR SCORE: ___ %
```

▶ Week 3: Test your progress

1 Podemos comprar sellos en el estanco, ¿verdad?
2 ¿Ha visto el tenis en la tele? Sí, he visto todo.
3 Era muy amable, como siempre.
4 ¡Madre mía! ¡Los huevos están rotos! No importa.
5 Ayer era un día bastante bueno.
6 El periódico inglés no era barato.
7 Creo que he visto una tintorería en El Corte Inglés.
8 ¿Hasta qué hora tiene que trabajar? ¿Hasta las ocho?
9 ¿A qué hora tenemos que ir? No puedo ir hasta más tarde.
10 En noviembre siempre hace mal tiempo en Manchester.
11 ¿Qué ha comprado? ¿Seis botellas de vino tinto? ¡Estupendo!
12 Talla cuarenta y cuatro: ¿qué es eso en inglés? Quizás catorce.
13 Hace mucho frío en esta casa. Tengo que comprar algo.
14 Primero he ido de compras y después hemos comido con amigos.
15 Hemos tenido la nueva tele desde ayer. ¡Y hoy está rota!
16 Ha comprado una maleta negra, no roja ¿verdad?
17 Todo era muy caro. Entonces no hemos comprado nada.
18 ¿Quién es el dependiente? Dónde está la leche?
19 No tenemos la camiseta en verde y al mismo precio.
20 Quisiera comprar algo para mí. Pero no demasiado caro.

YOUR SCORE: ___ %

▶ Week 4: Test your progress

1 ¿Qué ha dicho? Ha dicho: '¿Para quién son las patatas fritas?'
2 ¿Puede venir a nuestra casa? ¿La semana que viene?
3 Dice que la salida de la tienda está arriba, detrás del bar.
4 ¿Ha dicho que ha ido a Inglaterra?
5 ¿Qué quiere? Es que… estoy enfermo y no puedo trabajar.
6 ¿Podría ayudarme, por favor? ¿Hay un doctor aquí?
7 ¿Va a la cita sin zapatos? Esto no se puede hacer.
8 Conozco a Isabel Romero. Es una señora muy interesante.
9 Nadie puede beber quince cervezas en una noche. No es posible.
10 El postre me gusta mucho. Quisiera el helado.
11 Dice que es una cosa importante pero no tiene tiempo.
12 Hemos terminado y ahora tenemos que ir a Valencia.
13 Como muchas ensaladas. ¿Qué come usted?
14 ¿Cómo le gusta el pescado? ¿Sin ajo?
15 El nombre de esta verdura: ¿cómo se dice… en español?
16 No hay tiendas delante de la iglesia o detrás. ¿Qué hacemos?

17 Ha llamado la empresa. Un Señor López ha dicho que es una cosa importante.
18 Estoy seguro de que tienen agua con gas. La tienen siempre.
19 Dice que tiene dolores desde ayer. ¿Lo cree?
20 Tengo un resfriado. No puedo ir a Inglaterra hoy.

> YOUR SCORE: ___ %

▶ Week 5: Test your progress

1 Este coche no me gusta. El otro coche era mejor.
2 ¿Cuánto es/cuesta el billete – sólo ida?
3 ¿Qué ha dicho? Hable más despacio, por favor.
4 Esperamos comprar la gasolina más barata en España.
5 Está prohibido fumar en el metro.
6 ¿Es esto correcto? ¿Un buzón amarillo? No lo he sabido.
7 ¿Puedo hablar con el taller? Estamos a treinta kilómetros de Madrid.
8 ¿Qué es más lento? ¿El tren o el coche en la autovía?
9 No ha visto el semáforo, y ahora están en el hospital.
10 Hay una farmacia en la carretera, en la parada de autobús.
11 Quisiera dos billetes de ida y vuelta, no fumadores.
12 El problema con ella es que fuma demasiado.
13 Ha venido aquí, al final de la vía.
14 Hay mucha lluvia en Inglaterra. Estoy contento de estar en España.
15 Dicen que el río está a cinco minutos de la estación.
16 Si no me da el dinero voy a la policía.
17 Esta es la última gasolinera. ¿Tenemos suficiente agua y aceite?
18 Vienen en julio. No comprendo por qué Pedro viene más tarde.
19 Hablo con él ahora. Tengo un móvil.
20 No ha comido nada porque tiene dolor de cabeza.

> YOUR SCORE: ___ %

▶ Week 6: Test your progress

1 Me gusta escribir cartas, porque tengo un nuevo ordenador.
2 ¿Qué tal? ¿Qué pasa? ¿Puedo ayudarle?
3 La gente en la empresa es bastante aburrida.
4 No tengo el número de su móvil, lo siento.
5 ¿Le gusta la Sierra Nevada? Este año hemos tenido mucha nieve.
6 La segunda maleta está en el autobús. ¿Ha visto el bolso negro?
7 ¿Cuántas tarjetas ha escrito en Navidad? ¿Ochenta y ocho?

8 Esto es terrible. No han comido durante cinco días.

9 ¿Por qué no ha llamado por teléfono? Hemos esperado desde ayer.

10 Cuando lleguemos tomamos una copa – o dos.

11 ¿No lo sabe? El aeropuerto está abierto siempre – día y noche.

12 Estamos seguros de que lo ha hecho.

13 Hemos trabajado muchos años pero nunca en un barco.

14 He dado mi coche a mi hijo. Está muy contento.

15 Su madre es muy amable y hace una paella estupenda.

16 ¿Vive usted en un piso o en una casa en Torremolinos?

17 Tenemos que trabajar muchas horas. Cuatro hijas cuestan mucho.

18 ¿Lo puede reparar el taller? Espero que sí.

19 Lo conozco. Siempre va de compras con su perro.

20 ¿Quién ha dicho que no se puede fumar aquí?

21 Vamos a Dallas en avión. Luego vamos a Las Vegas en coche.

22 Quisiera hablar con el dependiente. No me ha dado la cuenta.

23 Hemos bebido su vino pero hemos venido hoy con dos botellas más.

24 Lo siento, pero **Instant Spanish** ha terminado ahora.

YOUR SCORE: ____ %

Week 6: Say it simply

1 Perdone, hay un problema con el coche. ¿Puede venir, por favor? Esto, detrás de la puerta, aquí a la izquierda. Yo no lo he hecho. No quisiera tener un problema más tarde.

2 Hola, buenos días, soy Kate Walker. El número de mi habitación es el 32. Llamo del aeropuerto. Tengo unas cosas en la habitación y ahora vamos a Birmingham. Lo siento, pero ¿puede ayudarme por favor? Tengo que tener las cosas. El hotel sabe dónde vivo en Birmingham. Muchas gracias.

Week 6: Spot the keys

1 It depends on the time you are going to leave. Normally it takes about 20 minutes but if we leave in the rush hour and there is a lot of traffic and a traffic-jam on the bridge over the river, you have to calculate some 45 or 50 minutes. The price is shown on the metre. Normally it costs between €20 and €25.

2 They have of course been in England!

how to use the flash cards

The **Flash cards** have been voted the best part of this course! Learning words and sentences can be tedious but with flash cards it's quick and good fun.

This is what you do:

When the **Day-by-day guide** tells you to use the cards cut them out. There are 22 **Flash words** and 10 **Flash sentences** for each week. Each card has a little number on it telling you to which week it belongs, so you won't cut out too many cards at a time or muddle them up later on.

First try to learn the words and sentences by looking at both sides. Then, when you have a rough idea start testing yourself – that's the fun bit. Look at the English, say the Spanish, and then check. Make two piles: 'correct' and 'wrong' or 'don't know'. When all the cards are used up, start again with the 'wrong' pile and try to whittle it down until you get all of them right. You can also play it 'backwards' by starting with the Spanish face up.

Keep the cards in a little box or put an elastic band around them. Take them with you on the bus, the train, to the hairdresser's or the dentist. If you find the paper too flimsy, photocopy the words and sentences onto card before cutting them up. You could also buy some plain card and stick them on or simply copy them out.

The 22 **Flash words** of each lesson are there to start you off. Convert the rest of the **New words** to **Flash cards**, too.

It's well worth it!

**Flash cards for Instant learning:
Don't lose them – use them!**

tenemos	¿qué tal?
vamos	voy
he estado	para
en casa	trabajo
he trabajado	ahora
estamos / somos	tengo

how are you? 1	we have 1
I go 1	we go, we are going, let's go 1
for 1	I have been, I was 1
I work 1	at home 1
now 1	I have worked 1
I have 1	we are 1

tiene [1]	siempre [1]
está / es [1]	también [1]
de vacaciones [1]	desgraciada- mente [1]
con [1]	cuesta/ cuestan [1]
el dinero [1]	ahora [1]
a la derecha [2]	a la izquierda [2]

always ¹	he/she/it has, you have ¹
also ¹	he/she/it is, you are ¹
unfortunately ¹	on holiday ¹
it costs, they cost ¹	with ¹
now ¹	the money ¹
on the left ²	on the right ²

algo 2	caro/cara 2
cerca 2	comer 2
¿cuánto…? 2	¿dónde…? 2
el desayuno 2	estupendo/a 2
hay 2	ir 2
la cuenta 2	luego 2

expensive ²	something ²
(to) eat ²	near ²
where…? ²	how much…? ²
great ²	the breakfast ²
(to) go ²	there is, there are ²
then, afterwards ²	the bill ²

muy **2**	puedo **2**
podemos **2**	quisiéramos **2**
menos **2**	el marido **2**
malo **2**	los servicios **2**
primero **3**	un cajero (automático) **3**
el estanco **3**	correos **3**

I can **2**	very **2**
we would like (to) **2**	we can **2**
the husband **2**	less **2**
the toilets **2**	bad **2**
a cash dispenser **3**	first **3**
the post office **3**	the tobacconist's **3**

3 comprar	3 los sellos
3 después	3 quizás
3 quisiera	3 tengo que
3 hasta	3 abierto/a
3 más tarde	3 los huevos
3 bastante	3 ayer

the stamps — (to) buy
perhaps — afterwards
I have to, I must — I would like (to)
open — until
the eggs — later
yesterday — enough

the stamps 3

(to) buy 3

perhaps 3

afterwards 3

I have to, I must 3

I would like (to) 3

open 3

until 3

the eggs 3

later 3

yesterday 3

enough 3

3 ¿quién?

3 un periódico

3 la farmacia

3 la mantequilla

3 creo

3 nuevo

4 el agua

4 alguien

4 arriba

4 delante (de)

4 detrás (de)

4 el pescado

3 a newspaper	**3** who?
3 the butter	**3** the pharmacy
3 new	**3** I believe
4 someone	**4** the water
4 in front of	**4** above, upstairs
4 the fish	**4** behind

4 está bien	4 ¿cómo?
4 la salida	4 me gusta
4 nadie	4 nuestro, nuestra
4 seguro	4 terminado
4 un resfriado	4 un vaso
4 una cosa	4 venir

4	4
how?	it's all right
I like	the exit
our	nobody
finished	sure
a glass	a cold
(to) come	a thing, matter

4 conozco (a)	**4** beber
4 un perro	**4** el dolor
5 la estación	**5** venga
5 la parada	**5** allí
5 abajo	**5** el buzón
5 hacer	**5** ¿por qué?

4 drink, to drink	**4** I know
4 the pain	**4** a dog
5 come, come on!	**5** the station
5 there	**5** the stop
5 the letter-box	**5** below, downstairs
5 why?	**5** (to) make, do

5 lleno	5 el otro, la otra
5 el coche	5 la calle
5 si	5 la gasolina
5 el taller	5 caliente
5 la lluvia	5 contento/a
5 el problema	5 comprendo

5 the other	**5** full
5 the street	**5** the car
5 the petrol	**5** if
5 hot	**5** the garage
5 pleased	**5** the rain
5 I understand	**5** the problem

5 el billete	5 ¿cuándo?
6 el aeropuerto	6 esperar
6 decir	6 en Navidad
6 la nieve	6 ¡qué lata!
6 ¡hombre!	6 ¿Le importaría?
6 veo	6 nunca

5	5
when?	the ticket

6	6
(to) wait	the airport

6	6
at Christmas	(to) say

6	6
what a bore!	the snow

6	6
would you mind?	well, hello!

6	6
never	I see

6	6
¿qué pasa?	¡espere!
6 el piso	**6** sé
6 saber	**6** la gente
6 llamar (por teléfono)	**6** conocemos
6 el libro	**6** el barco
6 hacen	**6** el año que viene

wait! ⁶	What is the matter? ⁶
I know ⁶	the flat, apartment ⁶
the people ⁶	(to) know ⁶
we know ⁶	to call (on the phone) ⁶
the boat, ship ⁶	the book ⁶
next year ⁶	they do, you do ⁶

Vamos a Madrid. 1

He estado en Marbella. 1

para mi empresa 1

Tengo una casa. 1

Tenemos dos niños. 1

Voy a casa. 1

Trabajo en Londres. 1

He trabajado mucho años. 1

El trabajo es bueno. 1

¿Está de vacaciones? 1

We go / let's go to Madrid. [1]

I have been / I was in Marbella. [1]

for my company [1]

I have a house. [1]

We have two children. [1]

I go, am going home. [1]

I work in London. [1]

I worked, have worked many years. [1]

The work is good. [1]

Are you / Is he, she on holiday? [1]

¿Tiene usted una habitación? 2

¿Dónde está la cafetería? 2

¿Cuánto cuesta? 2

¿Hay un banco aquí? 2

Quisiéramos ir a Marbella. 2

a las diez y media 2

La cuenta, por favor. 2

Tengo una tarjeta de crédito. 2

No puedo ir. 2

¿A qué hora podemos comer? 2

Do you have a room? 2

Where is the café? 2

How much does it cost? 2

Is there a bank here? 2

We would like to go to Marbella. 2

at half past ten 2

The bill, please. 2

I have a credit card. 2

I cannot go. 2

At what time can we eat? 2

Voy de compras.

3

Tengo que ir de compras.

3

Hace mal tiempo.

3

Lo siento.

3

He comprado demasiado.

3

No importa.

3

Quisiera comprar…

3

He ido al supermercado.

3

Tenemos que comprar…

3

¿Ha visto…?

3

I am going shopping. **3**

I must go shopping. **3**

It is bad weather. **3**

I am sorry. **3**

I have bought too much. **3**

It does not matter. **3**

I would like to buy… **3**

I have gone to the supermarket. **3**

We have to buy… **3**

Have you seen…? **3**

Alguien ha llamado. **4**

No ha dicho para qué. **4**

Es una cosa importante. **4**

La semana que viene
tenemos tiempo. **4**

Eso es posible. **4**

Me gusta mucho. **4**

El ajo no me gusta. **4**

¿Le gusta el hotel? **4**

¿Podría ayudarme, por
favor? **4**

¿Cómo se dice… en
español? **4**

Someone has called. 4

He/She did not say why. 4

It is an important matter. 4

We have time next week. 4

That is possible. 4

I like it very much. 4

I do not like garlic. 4

Do you like the hotel? 4

Can you help me please? 4

How do you say… in 4
Spanish?

dos billetes de ida y vuelta 5

Hable más despacio, 5
por favor.

¿Cuándo hay un tren? 5

Voy a hacer algo. 5

Estoy muy contento/a. 5

Esperamos que sí. 5

¿Dónde está la carretera? 5

¿Por qué lo compra? 5
¡Porque me gusta!

Hablo sólo un poco 5
español.

Si hay un coche, lo tomamos. 5

5

two return tickets

5

Please speak more slowly.

5

When is there a train?

5

I am going to do something.

5

I am very happy.

5

We hope so.

5

Where is the main road?

5

Why are you buying it?
Because I like it!

5

I only speak a little Spanish.

5

If there is a car we'll have it.

¿Qué tal sus vacaciones? 6

¿Le importaría ayudarme? 6

¿Le importaría darme…? 6

¿Qué pasa con…? 6

¡Vamos a tomar una copa! 6

No he ido nunca a Barcelona. 6

Tenemos que trabajar. ¡Qué lata! 6

He esperado durante una semana. 6

¿Qué ha hecho? 6

Tienen un piso. Lo sé. 6

How are/were your holidays? 6

Would you mind helping me? 6

Would you mind giving me...? 6

What's the matter with...? 6

Let's go and have a drink! 6

I've never been to Barcelona. 6

We must work. What a bore! 6

I waited for a week. 6

What did you do? 6

They have a flat.
I know that. 6

*This is to certify
that*

....

*has successfully completed
a six-week course of*

Instant Spanish

with .... results

Date   *Instructor*